THE
CANADIAN LIVING
RUSH-HOUR
COOKBOOK

THE CANADIAN LIVING RUSH-HOUR COOKBOOK

By Margaret Fraser and the food writers
of *Canadian Living* magazine

A RANDOM HOUSE/MADISON PRESS BOOK

Random House of Canada
1265 Aerowood Drive
Mississauga, Ontario
Canada
L4W 1B9

Canadian Cataloguing in Publication Data

Fraser, Margaret.
  The Canadian living rush-hour cookbook

Includes index.
ISBN 0-394-22088-9

1. Cookery. 2. Cookery, Canadian. I. Title.

TX715.F73 1989   641.5   C88-095152-4

Produced by
Madison Press Books
40 Madison Avenue
Toronto, Ontario
Canada
M5R 2S1

Printed in Italy

Contents

Introduction   6

30-Minute Meals   7

Appetizers, Sandwiches and Snacks   32

Soups and Salads   48

Beef, Pork, Lamb and Veal   68

Poultry   94

Fish and Seafood   108

Eggs and Cheese   120

Pasta, Rice and Grains   130

Vegetables   144

Desserts   152

Easy Meal-Planner   160

Tips for the Rush-Hour Cook   176

Acknowledgments and Credits   178

Index   181

Introduction

Everyone has a rush hour. No matter how organized we are or how well we plan ahead, sooner or later we all have to prepare dinner in a hurry. Here at *Canadian Living*, our food writers are some of the busiest people I know. And to cope with the rush-hour time squeeze they have developed wonderful recipes and ideas that show you how to beat the clock—and do it with style.

Quick meals can also be great meals. At *Canadian Living* we know that you don't just want it fast, you also want it to be tasty, nutritious and attractively presented. So in selecting the recipes, meal plans and timesaving ideas for this book, we made sure that every dish scores on all three counts.

We're also cooking fast "from scratch" using fresh ingredients, and there are no recipes that claim to take less than 45 minutes and then call for cold, cooked chicken, slivered rare roast beef or diced hard-cooked eggs.

Microwave ovens can be a godsend for the cook-in-a-hurry so we've also included alternative microwave directions for some of the recipes. Sidebars on every spread give you quick tips and ideas that we hope will become part of your kitchen repertoire.

Our opening section features 12 complete menus that can be made from start to table in 30 minutes or less. Each menu has a work schedule that shows you how to plan your kitchen time. And at the back of this cookbook the handy Meal-Planner mixes and matches our recipes to bring you 100 menus for all occasions—from dinners and brunches to suppers and lunches.

Best of all, we've carefully designed this book so that it can be picked up and *used* quickly. We picture you rushing home with a grocery bag under your arm and reaching for this book. Then we picture you sitting down to dinner half an hour later to a meal you'd be proud to serve at any time. Enjoy!

Margaret Fraser

6

30-Minute Meals

Here are twelve rush-hour menus, which can all be prepared in thirty minutes and prove that you don't have to sacrifice taste, presentation and variety to save time. We've even included mini work schedules to help you organize the meal preparation. Menus like Supper's in the Skillet (p. 24) and Dinner on Demand (p. 31) show you how to cook fast food with flair. And don't forget about the 100 menus in our Easy Meal-Planner at the back of this book for more fast and fabulous ideas.

Pasta-Pleaser

A late-night supper

Whether you're making a late-night dinner for friends or an after-work meal for the family, Linguine with Fresh Tomatoes and Seafood is a winner—especially in late summer when tomatoes are vine-ripened and juicy. Continue the Italian theme by dressing a salad of greens with an Italian-flavored vinaigrette (chart, p. 22). Dessert should be simple: fresh fruit and amaretti cookies.

LINGUINE WITH FRESH TOMATOES AND SEAFOOD*

TOSSED GREENS WITH PEPPERS

PARMESAN TOASTS*

FRESH FRUIT AND AMARETTI COOKIES
*Recipes appear on these two pages.

Linguine with Fresh Tomatoes and Seafood; Parmesan Toasts; tossed greens with peppers

---

LINGUINE WITH FRESH TOMATOES AND SEAFOOD

This delicious dish is featured on our cover. If the scallops are large, halve them crosswise.

1/3 cup	olive oil	75 mL
2	cloves garlic, minced	2
1/3 cup	finely chopped red onion	75 mL
1/2 lb	shrimp, peeled and deveined	250 g
1/2 lb	scallops	250 g
3/4 lb	linguine	375 g
3	tomatoes, seeded and diced	3
1/2 cup	chopped fresh basil	125 mL
	Salt and pepper	
2 tbsp	freshly grated Parmesan cheese	25 mL

• In large skillet, heat oil over medium-high heat; cook garlic, red onion, shrimp and scallops for 2 to 4 minutes or until shrimp are pink and scallops are opaque.
• Meanwhile, in large pot of boiling salted water, cook linguine until al dente (tender but firm). Drain and add to skillet; toss well.
• Add tomatoes and basil; toss well. Season with salt and pepper to taste. Sprinkle with Parmesan. Makes 4 servings.

WORK SCHEDULE

• **Bring pot of water to boil for pasta.**
• **Wash and spin-dry greens.**
• **Chop peppers for salad; chop tomatoes, onion, garlic and basil for sauce; chop garlic and parsley for toasts.**
• **Clean and rinse seafood.**

- **Spread bread for Parmesan Toasts.**
- **Cook pasta; make sauce while pasta cooks; broil toasts.**
- **Toss greens with vinaigrette (p. 22); toss pasta with sauce.**

PARMESAN TOASTS

These golden brown, crispy toasts are perfect with simple pasta dishes or as part of a light meal with soup or salad. Enjoy them as snacks, too!

2 tbsp	olive oil	25 mL
1	clove garlic, minced	1
8	thick slices 3/4-inch (2 cm) baguette (French stick), cut diagonally	8
1/4 cup	freshly grated Parmesan cheese	50 mL
1 tbsp	chopped fresh parsley	15 mL

- Combine olive oil and garlic; lightly brush some over one side of each bread slice.
- Arrange slices, garlic sides up; broil until golden brown.
- Turn slices and lightly brush with remaining oil mixture; sprinkle with Parmesan. Broil until cheese melts and toasts are golden brown. Sprinkle with parsley and serve warm. Makes 8 slices.

Classic and Easy

A dinner for unexpected company

Turn a simple everyday menu into company fare—with style. The soup, easily made with frozen carrots, can be served while the chicken cooks in the oven. Stir-fry the vegetables while plates are cleared for the main course. Instead of the soup, you can prepare a rice side dish on the stove-top or in the microwave oven.

CREAM OF CARROT SOUP
(recipe, p. 53)

ROSEMARY AND MUSTARD GLAZED CHICKEN*

VEGETABLE SAUTÉ
(recipe, p. 146)

STRAWBERRIES ROMANOFF
or
FAST FRUIT BRÛLÉE
(chart, p. 155)
*Recipe appears on this page.

WORK SCHEDULE

- **Set oven for chicken.**
- **Prepare vegetables for sauté and soup.**
- **Prepare chicken for oven; set aside.**
- **Hull and rinse berries; sprinkle with sugar and liqueur.**
- **Start soup; put chicken in oven.**
- **Finish and serve soup.**
- **Stir-fry vegetables as soup bowls are removed.**
- **Whip cream; finish dessert.**

ROSEMARY AND MUSTARD GLAZED CHICKEN

It takes only seconds to put together this glaze. Present the chicken on a platter surrounded by colorful sautéed vegetables.

1/4 cup	butter, melted	50 mL
1/4 cup	Dijon mustard	50 mL
1/4 cup	honey	50 mL
2 tsp	crumbled dried rosemary	10 mL
Pinch	pepper	Pinch
2-1/2 lb	chicken pieces	1.25 kg

- In small bowl or measure, combine butter, mustard, honey, rosemary and pepper.
- Arrange chicken, skin side down, on greased foil-lined baking sheet; brush with half of the mustard mixture. Bake in 400°F (200°C) oven for 20 minutes. Turn chicken over; brush with remaining mustard mixture. Bake for about 15 minutes longer or until skin is golden brown and chicken is no longer pink inside. Makes 4 servings.

Rosemary and Mustard Glazed Chicken; Vegetable Sauté; Cream of Carrot Soup

Better-Than-Take-Out

A kid-pleasing dinner

(In mug) Tomato Bouillon; Parmesan Fish Fingers with Lemon; potato croquettes; marinated cherry tomatoes

Who needs take-out when this delicious, nutritious version of fish fingers can be made easily in minutes. Give this everyday supper a special touch by serving colorful mugs of Tomato Bouillon or Spicy Clamato Bisque (recipe, p. 55) before or with the meal. In summer a frosted glass of Chilled Cucumber Soup (recipe, p. 55) is a quick addition. Cook frozen potato croquettes or puffs if you like.

TOMATO BOUILLON*

PARMESAN FISH FINGERS WITH LEMON*

POTATO CROQUETTES

MARINATED CHERRY TOMATOES

LIME SHERBET AND COOKIES
Recipes appear on opposite page.

TOMATO BOUILLON

This warming broth is perfect served in mugs in front of the fireplace after a day of skiing.

2 cups	water	500 mL
1	can (14 oz/ 398 mL) tomato sauce	1
1	can (10 oz/ 284 mL) consommé	1
1-1/2 cups	tomato juice	375 mL
2 tsp	grated lime rind	10 mL
1 tsp	granulated sugar	5 mL
1 tsp	drained prepared horseradish	5 mL
1/2 tsp	dried tarragon	2 mL
1/2 tsp	dried basil	2 mL
1/4 cup	dry red wine (optional)	50 mL
	Pepper	
	Croutons	
	Fresh watercress or parsley	

• In large saucepan, combine water, tomato sauce, consommé, tomato juice, lime rind, sugar, horseradish, tarragon and basil. Heat over medium heat for 10 minutes or until steaming hot; stir in wine (if using), and pepper to taste.
• Ladle into mugs or bowls, top with croutons and garnish with watercress. Makes about 6 cups (1.5 L).

WORK SCHEDULE

• **Set oven for fish fingers and potato croquettes (if using).**
• **Marinate tomatoes in vinaigrette (p. 22).**
• **Start bouillon.**
• **Prepare fish fingers; set aside before baking.**
• **Add frozen potato croquettes (if using) to pan.**
• **Bake fish and potatoes.**

PARMESAN FISH FINGERS WITH LEMON

All family members will love this version of a fast-food treat. Try the easy chicken variation for a change.

1 lb	fish fillets (thawed if frozen)	500 g
1/3 cup	fine dry bread crumbs	75 mL
1/3 cup	freshly grated Parmesan cheese	75 mL
1/2 tsp	paprika	2 mL
1	egg, lightly beaten	1
1 tbsp	butter, melted	15 mL
	Salt and pepper	
	Lemon wedges	

• Cut each fillet into strips about 3 inches (8 cm) long and 1/2 inch (1 cm) wide.
• In shallow dish, mix together bread crumbs, Parmesan and paprika. Dip each strip into beaten egg, then into bread crumb mixture. Place fish fingers on lightly greased baking sheet; lightly drizzle with butter.
• Bake in 450°F (230°C) oven for 7 to 10 minutes or until fish flakes easily when tested with fork. Season with salt and pepper to taste. Serve with lemon wedges. Makes 4 servings.

VARIATION:

PARMESAN CHICKEN FINGERS WITH LEMON:
• Substitute 4 chicken breasts (about 1-1/2 lb/750 g), skinned, boned and cut into 1/2-inch (1 cm) wide strips for the fish. Proceed as above, baking chicken fingers for about 6 minutes on one side and an additional 4 to 6 minutes on the other, or until crisp on the outside and cooked through. Makes 4 servings.

Friday Night with Friends

A stylish supper

Get the weekend off to a wonderful start with a simple dinner for friends. Serve assorted cheeses and crispbread crackers while dinner is in the works. Veal makes an elegant entrée, but for budget days substitute pork or lamb cutlets or even turkey scallopini. Finish the dinner with Speedy Mousse or fresh berries and cream.

ASSORTED CHEESES WITH CRISPBREAD CRACKERS

VEAL SCALLOPS WITH LEEKS AND LEMON MARMALADE*

SAUTÉED SNOW PEAS AND CHERRY TOMATOES
(recipe, p. 149)

SPEEDY MOUSSE*
*Recipes appear on these two pages.

Assorted cheeses with crispbread crackers; Veal Scallops with Leeks and Lemon Marmalade; Sautéed Snow Peas and Cherry Tomatoes

VEAL SCALLOPS WITH LEEKS AND LEMON MARMALADE

You can use boneless pork cutlets or boneless chicken breasts instead of the veal. Use homemade marmalade, if possible, and if you have lemon marmalade, use 2 tbsp (25 mL) of it instead of the combination of lemon juice and orange marmalade called for here.

1/4 cup	(approx) butter	50 mL
2 tbsp	vegetable oil	25 mL
1-1/2 lb	veal scallops	750 g
	Salt and pepper	
2	leeks (white parts only), chopped	2
1	small sweet red pepper, slivered	1
1/4 cup	dry sherry	50 mL
1/4 cup	chicken stock	50 mL
1 tbsp	lemon juice	15 mL
1 tbsp	orange marmalade	15 mL
1/4 cup	whipping cream	50 mL
	Chopped fresh parsley	

• In large skillet, heat butter and oil over medium heat; brown veal on both sides. Season with salt and pepper to taste; reduce heat and cook until veal is juicy and slightly pink in centre. Transfer to platter and keep warm in 200°F (100°C) oven.

• Add leeks and red pepper to pan, adding more butter if necessary; cook for 5 minutes or until tender.

• Stir in sherry, stock, lemon juice and marmalade; bring to boil, stirring to scrape up brown bits from bottom of pan; cook until sauce is slightly reduced. Whisk in cream; simmer for 2 minutes. Season with salt and pepper to taste. Pour sauce over veal. Sprinkle with parsley. Makes 4 servings.

SPEEDY MOUSSE

WORK SCHEDULE

- **Set out cheese and crackers.**
- **Prepare mousse; refrigerate.**
- **Prepare all vegetables.**
- **Measure remaining ingredients.**
- **Prepare veal.**
- **Cook peas; add tomatoes; heat through.**

Change the flavor of this mousse to suit your taste or the ingredients on hand. Use orange juice with orange, lemon or lime sherbet; use reconstituted raspberry or strawberry juice with raspberry or strawberry sherbet. Serve with crisp sugar cookies.

1	envelope unflavored gelatin	1
1/4 cup	cold water	50 mL
1/2 cup	fruit juice	125 mL
2 cups	sherbet	500 mL
1/2 cup	whipping cream, whipped	125 mL

- In blender, sprinkle gelatin over cold water; let stand for a few minutes to soften.
- Heat fruit juice to boiling. Pour into blender and process until gelatin is dissolved. Drop sherbet by spoonfuls into blender, blending after each addition.
- Using lowest speed, fold whipped cream into sherbet mixture. Pour into 4 parfait glasses and chill until set, about 30 minutes. Makes 4 servings.

Saturday Night Nibbling

An easy fondue party

Entertaining on short notice can be relaxed and fun. When guests arrive, give them a glass of wine and bring them into the kitchen. Break out the chopping boards and while you chat, get your friends to work—cubing bread, melting cheese, slicing sausages. Be sure to pass the Antipasto Platter as soon as your would-be chefs have it ready.

ANTIPASTO PLATTER*

FONDUE WITH ITALIAN FLAVORS*

MIXED GREENS WITH VINAIGRETTE
(chart, p. 22)

ICE CREAM AND ASSORTED TOPPINGS
(sidebar and recipes, p. 159)
Recipes appear on these two pages.

Recipes appear on these two pages.

FONDUE WITH ITALIAN FLAVORS

Here's an easy entertaining main dish that lends itself to good conversations while guests dip and enjoy. Add any favorite raw vegetables you wish to the list.

1-1/2 lb	sweet Italian sausages, salami or combination	750 g
1	loaf Italian bread	1
2	sweet red or green peppers	2
2 cups	cherry tomatoes	500 mL
FONDUE:		
3 cups	dry white wine	750 mL
1/2 cup	dried wild mushrooms	125 mL
1/2 lb	Fontina cheese, shredded	250 g
1/2 lb	sharp white Cheddar cheese, shredded	250 g
3 tbsp	all-purpose flour	50 mL
1	clove garlic, halved	1
1/2 cup	freshly grated Parmesan cheese	125 mL
	Pepper (optional)	

- Cut sausages, bread and peppers into 1-inch (2.5 cm) chunks. Set aside.
- **Fondue:** In saucepan, heat 1 cup (250 mL) of the wine almost to boiling; pour over mushrooms and soak for 30 minutes or until softened.
- Toss Fontina and Cheddar with flour until evenly coated. Rub fondue pot with garlic halves; discard garlic. Pour remaining wine into pot and heat over medium-low heat.
- Add cheese mixture to pot, a handful at a time, stirring until melted. Stir in Parmesan and mushrooms along with soaking liquid. Season with pepper (if using).
- Meanwhile, in skillet, cook sausages until no longer pink. Place on serving platter along with bread, peppers and tomatoes. Serve with fondue for dipping. Makes about 6 servings.

WORK SCHEDULE

With a little help from your friends . . .
- **Cut vegetables, melon wedges, etc. Drizzle with vinaigrette and herbs.**
- **Cut bread and cook sausage chunks for fondue.**
- **Grate cheese and make fondue.**
- **Make salad and set out dishes of toppings for ice cream.**

Fondue with Italian Flavors; Antipasto Platter

ANTIPASTO PLATTER

Your guests will enjoy helping themselves to this colorful appetizer platter. The fruit can be omitted to make a simple vegetable platter.

4	carrots, julienned	4
2	sweet green peppers, cut in rings	2
2	tomatoes, cut in wedges	2
1	seedless cucumber, cut in wedges	1
1	avocado	1
1	small cantaloupe	1
1/4 lb	thinly sliced salami	125 g
1/2 cup	black olives	125 mL

MARINADE:

1/3 cup	olive oil	75 mL
2 tbsp	red wine vinegar	25 mL
1 tbsp	lemon juice	15 mL
1	small clove garlic, minced	1
1/4 tsp	Dijon mustard	1 mL
Pinch	each dried basil, chervil and oregano	Pinch

• **Marinade:** Combine oil, vinegar, lemon juice, garlic, mustard, basil, chervil and oregano; mix well. Place carrots, green peppers, tomatoes and cucumber in bowl and pour marinade over. Cover and marinate for 20 minutes or refrigerate for up to 24 hours.

• Just before serving, peel and pit avocado; cut into wedges. Peel cantaloupe; cut into wedges.

• Drain vegetables, reserving marinade. Dip avocado wedges into marinade and roll up in slices of salami. Arrange on serving platter along with cantaloupe wedges, olives and marinated vegetables. Makes about 6 servings.

Meatless and Marvelous

A spur-of-the-moment brunch

Impress your family or guests by whipping up made-to-order omelettes rolled around sour cream and slivers of smoked salmon. Nothing could be faster or easier for an impromptu brunch or light dinner. Offer a fresh salad of greens and crisp toasted English muffin wedges. Finish with a simple dessert of Fresh Fruit in Yogurt.

SMOKED FISH AND SOUR CREAM OMELETTE*

ORANGE, OLIVE AND ONION SALAD
(recipe, p. 64)

TOASTED ENGLISH MUFFINS

FRESH FRUIT IN YOGURT
(recipe, p. 158)
*Recipe appears on opposite page.

BASIC FRENCH OMELETTE

Try this basic omelette with any of the fillings below or create your own variations.

3	**eggs**	**3**
1 tsp	**light cream**	**5 mL**
Pinch	**each salt and pepper**	**Pinch**
2 tsp	**butter**	**10 mL**

• In bowl, lightly beat together eggs, cream, salt and pepper.
• In 8-inch (20 cm) omelette pan, melt butter over high heat just until foaming; pour in egg mixture. Stir gently with fork to expose as much egg as possible to heat; cook until underside has set. With spatula lift edge of the omelette and tilt pan so uncooked eggs flow underneath and set. Repeat lifting and tilting 4 times around pan.
• When centre is still creamy but not runny, use fork to fold one-third of the omelette over centre. Tilt pan and lift-roll omelette over remaining one-third of omelette. Keep tilted pan over heat for 15 seconds to seal edges. Roll out omelette onto warmed serving plate. Makes 1 serving.

WORK SCHEDULE
• **Wash and spin-dry greens.**
• **Slice oranges and onions; cut olives in half.**
• **Mix dressing; set aside.**
• **Prepare dessert.**
• **Assemble ingredients for omelettes; make omelettes one at a time.**
• **Meanwhile, toast muffins; cut in wedges.**
• **Arrange salad; drizzle with dressing.**

VARIATIONS:

SMOKED FISH AND SOUR CREAM OMELETTE:
• Before folding and rolling each omelette as described in Basic French Omelette, spread 1 tbsp (15 mL) sour cream in row across omelette parallel to fold. Sprinkle cream with 2 tbsp (25 mL) flaked salmon, trout or whitefish, or 1 tbsp (15 mL) finely chopped smoked salmon.

HERBED OMELETTE:
• Add 1 tsp (5 mL) each chopped fresh parsley and chives (or green onion) plus 1/4 tsp (1 mL) dried tarragon to uncooked egg mixture.

CHEESE OMELETTE:
• Sprinkle 1/4 cup (50 mL) shredded cheese (Cheddar, Gruyère or Fontina) over each omelette before rolling.

LEEK AND CREAM FILLING:

3 cups	**finely sliced leeks (white and light green parts only)**	**750 mL**
2 tbsp	**chicken stock or water**	**25 mL**
2 tbsp	**whipping cream**	**25 mL**
1 tbsp	**butter**	**15 mL**
	Salt and pepper	

• In saucepan, cover and cook leeks and stock over medium-low heat until leeks are softened, 12 to 15 minutes.
• Uncover and cook over high heat, stirring almost constantly, until moisture has evaporated. Add cream, butter, and salt and pepper to taste. Keep warm.

• Spread omelette with one-quarter of the filling in row parallel to fold. Fold and roll as described in Basic French Omelette. Makes enough for 4 omelettes.

PROVENÇALE FILLING:

1 tbsp	**olive oil**	**15 mL**
1/2 cup	**chopped onions**	**125 mL**
1/4 cup	**finely chopped sweet green pepper**	**50 mL**
Half	**clove garlic, minced**	**Half**
1/2 cup	**finely cubed zucchini**	**125 mL**
1 cup	**drained canned plum or coreless tomatoes**	**250 mL**
1/4 tsp	**dried oregano**	**1 mL**
2 tsp	**chopped pitted black olives**	**10 mL**
	Salt and pepper	

• In small saucepan, heat oil over medium heat; cook onions, green pepper and garlic until tender, about 3 minutes.
• Stir in zucchini, tomatoes and oregano; cook, uncovered, for 10 minutes or until thickened, breaking up tomatoes with wooden spoon and stirring occasionally. Stir in olives, and salt and pepper to taste; keep warm.
• Spread omelette with 2 tbsp (25 mL) of the filling in row parallel to fold. Fold and roll as described in Basic French Omelette. Makes enough for 4 omelettes.

Smoked Fish and Sour Cream Omelette

Fast Food with Flair

A tasty, timesaving family dinner

Lemon-Basil Chicken Strips can be elegant fare when presented on beautiful china or everyday-casual on bright chunky plates. If you're really pressed for time, save the vegetables for another occasion and simply serve the rotini and salad side dishes.

LEMON-BASIL CHICKEN STRIPS*
VEGETABLE MEDLEY
PARMESAN ROTINI*
SPINACH, CASHEW AND RED ONION SALAD
PEARS AND BRIE

*Recipes appear on this page.

LEMON-BASIL CHICKEN STRIPS

Basil, lemon and soy sauce add lots of flavor to these tender chicken strips.

4	boneless skinless chicken breasts	4
1 tbsp	dried basil	15 mL
	Pepper	
2 tbsp	soy sauce	25 mL
2 tbsp	lemon juice	25 mL
2 tbsp	vegetable oil	25 mL

• Slice chicken into 2-inch (5 cm) long strips about 1/2 inch (1 cm) wide. Pat basil, and pepper to taste onto chicken.
• In bowl, combine soy sauce, lemon juice and oil; add chicken, stirring to coat well. Place slices in single layer on foil-lined broiler rack. Let stand for 5 minutes.
• Broil chicken 4 inches (10 cm) from heat for 4 to 5 minutes or until tender and no longer pink inside. Makes 4 servings.

PARMESAN ROTINI

Here's an easy pasta side dish to complement a chicken, beef or pork entrée.

1/2 lb	rotini	250 g
2 tbsp	butter, softened	25 mL
1/4 cup	(approx) freshly grated Parmesan cheese	50 mL
2 tbsp	sour cream	25 mL
	Salt and pepper	

• In large pot of boiling salted water, cook rotini according to package directions or until al dente (tender but firm); drain well.
• Toss rotini with butter, Parmesan cheese and sour cream. Season with salt and pepper to taste. Pass extra Parmesan cheese separately, if desired. Makes 4 side-dish servings.

WORK SCHEDULE

• **Bring pot of water to boil for pasta.**
• **Wash spinach; slice onion; mix dressing.**
• **Prepare chicken; let stand before cooking.**
• **Cook rotini; steam or microwave frozen vegetables.**
• **Broil chicken; finish rotini; toss salad with dressing.**

Lemon-Basil Chicken Strips; Parmesan Rotini; Vegetable Medley

Easy Summertime Grilling

A supper al fresco

When the weather is warm and the evenings are long, you don't want to be in the kitchen. Here's a quick meal that shows off the bounty of the season. Choose turkey scallopini to grill quickly on the gas barbecue (you'll need a bit more time for a charcoal barbecue). A simple vinaigrette can dress both a green salad and beefsteak tomato slices topped with sliced green onions. All you need for a finale is a bowl of plump blueberries or freshly picked strawberries.

Herb-Grilled Turkey Scallopini; corn-on-the-cob; sliced beefsteak tomatoes; Greens with Vinaigrette

---

HERB-GRILLED TURKEY SCALLOPINI*

SLICED BEEFSTEAK TOMATOES

CORN-ON-THE-COB

GREENS WITH VINAIGRETTE*

FRESH BERRIES AND CHOCOLATE WAFERS
Recipes appear on these two pages.

VINAIGRETTE FOR GREENS

You can vary the flavor of this dressing by changing the vinegar or the oil. Substitute lemon juice, balsamic or fruit-flavored vinegars (raspberry, strawberry) or herbed vinegars (tarragon, basil) for half the vinegar called for. Use olive oil instead of vegetable oil, or substitute a strong-flavored oil (like walnut) for 1 tbsp (15 mL) of the vegetable oil.

In 1-cup (250 mL) measure, whisk together vinegar, oil, and honey, mustard and options (if using). Season with salt and pepper to taste. Quickly pour over torn salad greens; toss and serve. Makes about 3/4 cup (175 mL) dressing.

	Vinegar	Oil	Honey	Dijon Mustard	Options
Classic	1/4 cup (50 mL) white wine or cider vinegar	2/3 cup (150 mL) vegetable	1 tsp (5 mL)	1 tsp (5 mL)	—
Italian-flavored	1/4 cup (50 mL) red wine vinegar	2/3 cup (150 mL) olive oil	—	—	1/2 tsp (2 mL) dried basil 1/4 tsp (1 mL) dried oregano 1 clove garlic
Tomato	1/4 cup (50 mL) white vinegar	2/3 cup (150 mL) vegetable	1 tsp (5 mL)	1 tsp (5 mL)	2 tbsp (25 mL) ketchup
Creamy	1/4 cup (50 mL) white vinegar	2/3 cup (150 mL) vegetable	1 tsp (5 mL)	1 tsp (5 mL)	1/3 cup (75 mL) sour cream, yogurt or mayonnaise

HERB-GRILLED TURKEY SCALLOPINI

WORK SCHEDULE

- **Marinate turkey scallopini.**
- **Wash berries.**
- **Put water on for corn; light barbecue.**
- **Wash spinach; slice red and green onions and tomatoes.**
- **Mix dressing; drizzle half on tomato slices.**
- **Cook corn and turkey.**
- **Toss salad with remaining dressing.**

If turkey scallopini aren't available, slice partially frozen turkey breast thinly, then pound between two sheets of waxed paper into 1/4-inch (5 mm) thick slices. Serve with corn-on-the-cob, sliced tomatoes and a spinach salad.

2 tbsp	olive oil	25 mL
2 tbsp	lemon juice	25 mL
3	cloves garlic, minced	3
1/2 tsp	each dried oregano, rosemary and thyme	2 mL
1/4 tsp	salt	1 mL
	Pepper	
1 lb	turkey scallopini	500 g

- In bowl, combine oil, lemon juice, garlic, oregano, rosemary, thyme, salt, and pepper to taste. Brush mixture over both sides of each turkey slice.
- Grill turkey on lightly greased grill over hot coals or on high setting for 2 minutes per side or just until cooked through. Makes about 4 servings.

Supper's in the Skillet

A speedy frittata dinner

Here's a super-quick one-skillet supper—with an easy cleanup to follow. Spend a little more time making a special dessert like Baked Winter Compote or Applesauce Angel Pudding (recipe, p. 152). Or make a Mushroom Consommé (sidebar, p. 52) to serve first. Choose a peasant-style bread—brown, coarse and preferably with seeds—broken into chunks to serve with the frittata.

ZUCCHINI, POTATO AND EGG SKILLET SUPPER*

LETTUCE AND TOMATO SALAD

WARM BREAD CHUNKS

BAKED WINTER COMPOTE*

*Recipes appear on these two pages.

BAKED WINTER COMPOTE

Here's a comforting fruit dessert to serve warm, garnished with sour cream, whipped cream or yogurt.

1	orange	1
1	can (14 oz/398 mL) pineapple chunks	1
1 cup	mixed dried fruits*	250 mL
1/4 cup	packed brown sugar	50 mL
1/2 tsp	cinnamon	2 mL
1/4 tsp	ground nutmeg	1 mL
	Sour cream, whipped cream or yogurt (optional)	

• Grate rind from orange and reserve; remove white pith, then cut orange into thin slices. Place orange rind and slices in 4-cup (1 L) casserole along with pineapple, dried fruits, sugar, cinnamon and nutmeg. Mix gently. Bake, covered, in 350°F (180°C) oven for about 30 minutes or until dried fruits are softened, stirring once or twice. Let cool slightly; serve with dollop of sour cream (if using). Makes 4 or 5 servings.
*Use packaged mixed dried fruits or any combination of dried figs, prunes, apricots and peaches.

• **Microwave Directions:** Grate rind from orange and reserve; remove white pith, then cut orange into thin slices. Drain pineapple, pouring juice in 8-cup (2 L) dish. Add orange rind, dried fruits, sugar, cinnamon and nutmeg. Microwave, covered, at High for 4 minutes, stirring once. Add reserved pineapple chunks and orange slices. Microwave, covered, at High for 2 minutes or until dried fruits are softened. Let stand for 5 minutes. Serve as above.

Zucchini, Potato and Egg Skillet Supper; lettuce and tomato salad

WORK SCHEDULE

• **Assemble compote; place in oven.**
• **Wash greens and tomatoes for salad.**
• **Grate zucchini; peel and dice potatoes.**
• **Chop chives or green onions.**
• **Cook frittata.**
• **Warm bread; toss salad.**

ZUCCHINI, POTATO AND EGG SKILLET SUPPER

You can whip up a tasty dinner in no time, using staples such as eggs and potatoes. A tossed lettuce and tomato salad and fresh bread complete the meal.

1/4 cup	butter or olive oil	50 mL
2	potatoes, peeled and diced	2
2-1/2 cups	coarsely grated (unpeeled) zucchini	625 mL
1/4 cup	chopped fresh chives or chopped green onions	50 mL
4	large eggs	4
	Salt and pepper	

• In 10-inch (25 cm) heavy skillet, melt half of the butter. Add potatoes; cook over medium heat, stirring, for about 5 minutes or until tender. Add zucchini and chives; cook, stirring, for 1 minute.

• In large bowl, beat eggs lightly; stir in vegetables. Season with salt and pepper to taste.

• Wipe out skillet and melt remaining butter; pour in egg mixture. Reduce heat to medium-low; cook, shaking pan occasionally, for about 5 minutes or until bottom is lightly browned. Cover and cook for 5 to 6 minutes longer or until top is firm. To serve, cut into wedges. Makes about 4 servings.

Heart-Smart and Healthy

A light but delightful dinner

Small, sliced loins of lamb make a beautiful presentation served in a red wine sauce. Complemented by fluffy rice, Romaine and Red Onion Salad and a light broiled dessert, this meal is also low in fat. If cooking with wine and sherry is not to your taste, substitute chicken stock in the lamb recipe and sprinkle orange juice on the grapefruit.

MEDALLIONS OF LAMB IN RED WINE SAUCE*

FLUFFY RICE

ROMAINE AND RED ONION SALAD*

MELBA TOAST OR SESAME BREADSTICKS

BROILED SHERRIED GRAPEFRUIT

*Recipes appear on these two pages.

ROMAINE AND RED ONION SALAD

Serve this light salad alongside Lamb Medallions in Red Wine Sauce. Add spinach or watercress to the romaine and red onion combination if you like.

1	head romaine lettuce, torn	1
1	red onion, thinly sliced	1
2 cups	spinach, torn (or 1 bunch watercress), optional	500 mL
3 tbsp	vegetable oil	50 mL
2 tbsp	lemon juice	25 mL
2 tbsp	orange juice	25 mL
1	clove garlic, minced	1
1/4 tsp	salt	1 mL
1/4 tsp	black pepper	1 mL
1/2 tsp	dry mustard	2 mL

• Toss together romaine, red onion and spinach (if using). Whisk together oil, lemon and orange juices, garlic, salt, pepper and mustard. Pour over salad and serve. Makes 4 servings.

WORK SCHEDULE

• **Halve grapefruits; loosen sections; sprinkle with sherry and sugar. Place on baking sheet; set aside.**
• **Start rice.**
• **Wash romaine; slice onion; mix dressing.**
• **Cook lamb.**
• **Toss salad; set out melba toast or breadsticks.**
• **Broil grapefruit while clearing dishes.**

Medallions of Lamb in Red Wine Sauce; fluffy rice; Romaine and Red Onion Salad

MEDALLIONS OF LAMB IN RED WINE SAUCE

Succulent lamb in a light wine sauce is impressive yet easy to make. Boneless lamb loins, like pork tenderloins, are fast-cooking meats when cut into slices first.

2	boneless lamb loins (about 1/2 lb/250 g each)	2
	Salt and pepper	
1	large clove garlic, crushed	1
1 tbsp	vegetable oil	15 mL
1/2 cup	dry red wine	125 mL
1/4 cup	chicken stock	50 mL
2 tsp	red currant jelly	10 mL

• With blade of knife almost parallel to meat, slice lamb diagonally across the grain into 1/2-inch (1 cm) thick slices; season with salt and pepper to taste. Set aside.

• In heavy skillet, cook garlic in oil over medium-low heat for 3 minutes. Remove and discard garlic. Increase heat to medium-high; cook lamb for about 2 minutes per side or until golden brown but still pink in centre. Remove lamb from skillet and keep warm.

• Add wine and stock to skillet; cook for about 2 minutes or until sauce is reduced by half, stirring occasionally. Add jelly and cook, stirring, for about 1 minute more or until incorporated into wine and stock. Place lamb on serving plates and spoon sauce over. Makes 4 servings.

Simple Elegance

A quick and classy salmon dinner

Steamed on the stove-top, salmon is quickly cooked and deliciously moist. The bulgur pilaf makes a pleasant yet nutritious change from rice or potatoes. You can reserve the snow peas for company and use only green beans if you're cooking an everyday supper. Fresh bunches of grapes, frozen for 20 minutes only, provide a refreshing end to the meal when served with mild cheese.

STEAMED SALMON FILLETS*
BULGUR AND MUSHROOM PILAF*
GREEN BEANS AND SNOW PEAS
CRISP FLATBREAD
FROSTED GRAPES AND CHEESE
*Recipes appear on this page.

STEAMED SALMON FILLETS

The flavorful Court Bouillon makes these steamed salmon fillets extra special. If you're too busy to make the Court Bouillon, use diluted chicken stock with the peppercorns and thyme. If you don't have a steamer basket, use a rack to hold the fish above the liquid.

1-1/2 lb	salmon fillets, skin removed	750 g
COURT BOUILLON:		
4 cups	water	1 L
1	carrot, chopped	1
1	stalk celery, chopped	1
1	onion, chopped	1
	Rind and juice of 1 lemon	
1/2 tsp	peppercorns	2 mL
1/2 tsp	dried thyme	2 mL
	Lemon wedges	

• **Court Bouillon:** In wok, large skillet or Dutch oven, combine water, carrot, celery, onion, lemon juice, lemon rind, peppercorns and thyme. Bring to boil; cover and boil for 10 minutes.
• Arrange salmon on plate; place plate in steamer basket and cover. Place steamer in wok and steam fish over boiling Court Bouillon for 10 minutes per inch (2.5 cm) of thickness or until fish is opaque and flakes easily when tested with fork. Serve with lemon wedges. Makes 4 servings.

BULGUR AND MUSHROOM PILAF

Bulgur (cracked wheat) is a grain that cooks quickly and can be used as you would rice.

2 tbsp	butter	25 mL
2 cups	thinly sliced mushrooms	500 mL
1	onion, chopped	1
2 cups	boiling water or chicken stock	500 mL
1 cup	bulgur	250 mL
1 tsp	dried basil	5 mL
	Salt and pepper	

• In large skillet, melt butter over medium heat; cook mushrooms and onion, stirring, for about 5 minutes or until tender.
• Stir in water, bulgur and basil; cover and simmer over low heat for 15 minutes or until liquid is absorbed. Season with salt and pepper to taste. Makes 4 servings.

WORK SCHEDULE
• **Cook bulgur pilaf.**
• **Cook beans and/or peas.**
• **Cook salmon; set out bread.**
• **Just before serving dinner, place grapes in freezer.**

Steamed Salmon Fillets; Bulgur and Mushroom Pilaf; green beans and snow peas

Dinner on Demand

An "eat-when-you're-ready-to" meal

For those nights when everyone in the household is eating at a different time—shopping, dates or you name it—here's the perfect solution. With easy-to-make Chicken and Snow Peas in Packets, each family member can finish cooking his or her supper as it's needed. A selection of finger food from your vegetable crisper and fruit or ice cream for dessert round out the meal.

CHICKEN AND SNOW PEAS IN PACKETS*

OVEN-BAKED FRENCH FRIES

VEGETABLE CRUDITÉS

ICE CREAM WITH FAST CHOCOLATE SAUCE*

*Recipes appear on this page.

WORK SCHEDULE

- **Set oven.**
- **Prepare chicken packets.**
- **Clean and cut crudités to leave in crisper.**
- **Make chocolate sauce.**
- **Leave clear, printed instructions for cooking chicken packets and reheating chocolate sauce for family members.**
- **To reheat chocolate sauce in microwave: Microwave at Medium-High (70%) for 45 to 60 seconds.**

CHICKEN AND SNOW PEAS IN PACKETS

Kids will love to open these surprise packages. Serve them with oven-baked French fries for an added treat.

3/4 lb	boneless skinless chicken breasts	375 g
2 tbsp	chopped fresh parsley	25 mL
1	small clove garlic, minced	1
1/4 lb	snow peas, trimmed	125 g
2 tbsp	butter	25 mL
	Salt and pepper	
2 tbsp	lemon juice	25 mL
	Lemon slices	

- Using palm of hand, flatten chicken breasts and place each breast on double thickness of foil about 8 inches (20 cm) square.
- Combine parsley and garlic; sprinkle over chicken. Arrange snow peas evenly on top. Dot with butter and season with salt and pepper to taste. Sprinkle with lemon juice. Fold up packets and seal.
- Place packets on ungreased baking sheet and bake in 350°F (180°C) oven for 20 to 25 minutes or until chicken is no longer pink inside. Transfer packets to plates and serve with lemon slices. Makes 2 or 3 servings.

FAST CHOCOLATE SAUCE

Here's an easy chocolate sauce to drizzle over ice cream or slices of angel food or pound cake.

1 cup	semisweet chocolate chips	250 mL
1/4 cup	corn syrup	50 mL
2 tbsp	strong coffee	25 mL
1 tbsp	butter	15 mL

- In saucepan, combine chocolate chips, corn syrup, coffee and butter over low heat, stirring occasionally. Heat just until chocolate is melted and sauce is hot. Keep warm over hot water. Makes about 1 cup (250 mL).
- **Microwave Directions:** In 2-cup (500 mL) measure, combine chocolate chips, corn syrup, coffee and butter. Microwave at Medium-High (70%) for 2 to 4 minutes or until chocolate is melted and sauce is warm and smooth, stirring once.

Chicken and Snow Peas in Packets; oven-baked french fries

Appetizers, Sandwiches and Snacks

Snappy appetizers and sandwiches are perfect for today's grazers, sudden snack-attacks or just simple, little meals. Speedy dips and spreads like Warm Cheddar Dip or Double-Olive Tuna Spread make spur-of-the-moment entertaining effortless. Use them as sandwich fillings, too. Hot sandwiches like Avocado Melts make a convenient alternative to take-out food. We've also included favorite snacks like pizza and tacos that can easily become the main course in fast no-fuss meals.

THREE-PEPPER THREE-CHEESE PIZZA

If chèvre is unavailable, any assertive cheese (including old Cheddar) will do nicely.

	Cornmeal	
4	unbaked pizza crusts* (about 6 in/15 cm each)	4
2 tbsp	olive oil	25 mL
1	clove garlic, minced	1
1	onion, sliced	1
3	small sweet peppers (green, red, yellow), cut in strips	3
8	small mushrooms, sliced	8
1/2 tsp	each chopped fresh basil and oregano (or pinch each dried)	2 mL
	Salt and pepper	
8	cooked or canned artichoke hearts (optional)	8
4	large plum tomatoes, sliced	4
1/3 lb	mozzarella cheese, sliced	175 g
1/2 cup	crumbled goat cheese (or 1 cup/ 250 mL shredded old Cheddar)	125 mL
1/4 cup	freshly grated Parmesan cheese	50 mL

- Sprinkle two lightly greased baking sheets with cornmeal; place pizza crusts on top and set aside.
- In skillet, heat oil; cook garlic and onion until softened but not browned. Add peppers and mushrooms; cook until slightly softened. Add basil and oregano; season with salt and pepper to taste. Add artichokes (if using).
- Around edge of each pizza crust, arrange alternate slices of tomato and mozzarella; spoon pepper mixture into centres. Sprinkle each with goat cheese and Parmesan. Bake near bottom of 450°F (220°C) oven for 10 to 15 minutes or until crust is well browned. Makes 4 servings.
*Make 4 individual crusts from any basic pizza dough. Alternatively, you can buy excellent unbaked dough at many Italian bakeries, takeouts and supermarkets.

(Clockwise from top) Crab Salad Croissant with Peaches and Pecans (p. 38); Three-Pepper Three-Cheese Pizza; Warm Pasta Seafood Salad (p. 61)

HUMMUS

Serve this Middle Eastern dip with fresh vegetables and warm pita bread. Easy to make, this dip is a good source of fibre and protein. Tahini (sesame seed paste) is available at many health food stores.

3	cloves garlic	3
1	can (19 oz/540 mL) chick-peas, drained	1
1/4 cup	tahini or peanut butter	50 mL
3 tbsp	lemon juice	50 mL
2 tbsp	vegetable oil	25 mL
2 tbsp	water	25 mL
1 tsp	cumin	5 mL
1/2 tsp	salt	2 mL

• In food processor, mince garlic. Add chick-peas, tahini, lemon juice, oil, water, cumin and salt; process until smooth. Taste and adjust seasoning if necessary. Transfer to serving bowl. Makes about 1-1/2 cups (375 mL).

GARLIC TOMATO CROSTINI

Spread a chunky garlic, tomato and Parmesan cheese topping over small rounds of French bread and serve in a napkin-lined basket with wine before dinner. Or spread it over larger slices of bread, melba toast or pita bread for lunch along with a green salad.

1	French stick (baguette)	1
1/4 cup	butter, melted	50 mL
TOPPING:		
2 tbsp	olive oil	25 mL
1 cup	finely chopped onions	250 mL
2	large cloves garlic, minced	2
1	can (28 oz/ 796 mL) tomatoes	1
2	egg yolks	2
1 cup	freshly grated Parmesan cheese	250 mL
	Salt and pepper	

• Cut bread diagonally into 1/2-inch (1 cm) thick slices. Place on baking sheet in single layer and brush with some of the melted butter. Broil for 3 minutes or until golden. Turn bread, brush with remaining butter and broil until golden.
• **Topping:** In large skillet, heat oil over medium heat; cook onions and 1 of the garlic cloves, stirring frequently, until onions are translucent and tender, about 5 minutes.
• Drain tomatoes (reserve juice for another use). Squeeze out seeds and chop pulp into 1/4-inch (5 mm) dice. Stir into skillet and cook over medium-high heat, stirring frequently, until sauce is thickened, 5 to 10 minutes.
• Remove from heat; stir in remaining garlic, egg yolks, cheese, and salt and pepper to taste.
• Spread tomato mixture over toast rounds and bake in 400°F (200°C) oven for 5 to 10 minutes or until heated through and topping is beginning to brown around edges. (For browner topping, broil crostini 4 inches/10 cm from heat.) Serve immediately. Makes 10 appetizer servings, 4 or 5 luncheon servings.

(Left to right) Mozzarella Toasts; Garlic Tomato Crostini

MOZZARELLA TOASTS

When everyone's too hungry to wait for even the fastest dinner, serve these easy appetizers while a main dish is cooking.

3 tbsp	butter, softened	50 mL
3	anchovy fillets, minced	3
1	small clove garlic, minced	1
8	slices (1/2 in/1 cm thick) French bread	8
8	slices (1/4 in/ 5 mm thick) mozzarella cheese	8
	Dried basil	

• Combine butter, anchovies and garlic, mixing well; spread on 1 side of each bread slice. Top each with cheese slice, trimming to fit bread. Sprinkle with basil to taste; broil until cheese is bubbly and melted. Makes 8 appetizers.

SPINACH DIP IN A RYE SHELL

This dip has almost become a classic, although there are several versions. The bread becomes the serving bowl and you can cut or tear the chunks removed to serve with the dip along with assorted vegetables.

1/4 lb	cream cheese	125 g
1/2 cup	mayonnaise	125 mL
1/2 cup	plain yogurt	125 mL
1	pkg (300 g) frozen chopped spinach, thawed	1
2	green onions, finely chopped	2
4	slices crisp cooked bacon, finely chopped	4
1	small clove garlic, minced	1
	Salt and pepper	
1	round loaf dark rye bread	1

• In bowl, beat cream cheese with mayonnaise until smooth; stir in yogurt. Squeeze excess water from spinach and chop finely; stir into cream cheese mixture. Add green onions, bacon and garlic; mix well. Season with salt and pepper to taste.
• Slice circle of crust from top of bread. Hollow out loaf, leaving shell at least 1 inch (2.5 cm) thick, and cutting or tearing removed bread into pieces to serve with dip. Spoon dip into hollowed-out bread. Makes about 2 cups (500 mL).

Spinach Dip in a Rye Shell

CREAMY BLUE CHEESE DIP

A bowl of blue cheese dip has become the "classic" partner to crispy chicken wings and crunchy side nibbles such as celery and carrot sticks, radishes and green onions. (photo, p. 103)

3/4 cup	sour cream	175 mL
3/4 cup	cottage cheese	175 mL
2 tbsp	crumbled blue cheese	25 mL
1	small clove garlic, minced	1
1/2 tsp	salt	2 mL
1 tbsp	chopped fresh chives	15 mL

• In food processor, process sour cream, cottage cheese, blue cheese, garlic and salt for 1 to 2 minutes or until smooth, scraping down side of work bowl once or twice. Add chives; process just until mixed. Makes about 1-3/4 cups (425 mL).

WARM CHEDDAR DIP

Keep carrot and celery sticks ready for after-school munching and for serving with easy-to-make dips such as this one. You can add 1 to 2 tbsp (15 to 25 mL) more taco sauce to the Warm Nacho Cheese Dip variation for extra heat.

1/4 cup	milk	50 mL
1/4 lb	cream cheese	125 g
1 cup	shredded Cheddar cheese	250 mL
1/2 tsp	dry mustard	2 mL
1/2 tsp	Worcestershire sauce	2 mL
Dash	hot pepper sauce	Dash
2	green onions, chopped	2

• In small saucepan, combine milk and cream cheese over low heat; whisk until blended and smooth. Increase heat to medium; stir in Cheddar until melted and smooth.
• Stir in mustard, Worcestershire, hot pepper sauce and half of the green onions; cook until heated through. Transfer to serving dish. Sprinkle with remaining green onion. Makes about 1 cup (250 mL).

VARIATION:

WARM NACHO CHEESE DIP:
• Stir 1/4 cup (50 mL) taco sauce into warm cheese dip before sprinkling with remaining green onion. Serve with nacho or taco chips or pita crisps. Makes about 1-1/4 cups (300 mL).

Banana Buttermilk Pancakes are great at any meal of the day. Serve them for breakfast with butter and maple syrup; for lunch with thickly sliced bacon; or for dinner with caramelized apple wedges with a side order of bacon, and a spinach salad with lemon vinaigrette.

BANANA BUTTERMILK PANCAKES

Little silver dollar pancakes are hard to resist.

1-1/2 cups	all-purpose flour	375 mL
2 tbsp	granulated sugar	25 mL
1 tsp	baking soda	5 mL
1/3 cup	chopped walnuts	75 mL
1 cup	mashed ripe bananas (about 2)	250 mL
2 cups	buttermilk	500 mL
2	eggs	2
1/4 cup	butter, melted	50 mL
	Butter for cooking	

• In large bowl, sift or stir together flour, sugar and baking soda; mix in walnuts.
• Combine bananas, buttermilk, eggs and butter; stir into dry ingredients just until moistened.
• In large skillet or griddle, melt just enough butter over medium heat to coat surface of pan. Pour in about 3 tbsp (50 mL) batter for each pancake; cook pancakes, in batches, for 1-1/2 to 2 minutes on one side or until tiny bubbles appear on surface and bottom is golden brown. Flip and cook second side for about 1 minute or until golden. Makes 4 to 6 servings.

FRENCH TOAST WITH PESTO

Pesto and cream cheese turn this familiar breakfast favorite into a delightful supper. Make double or triple batches of pesto and store them in the refrigerator for up to 3 days or in the freezer for up to 1 month. As a pasta sauce or omelette filling, pesto is very handy for the rush-hour cook.

1/4 lb	cream cheese, softened	125 g
8	slices bread	8
1/4 cup	Pesto (recipe follows)	50 mL
2	eggs	2
1/4 cup	milk	50 mL
1/4 cup	(approx) vegetable or olive oil	50 mL

PESTO:

1/2 cup	fresh basil or parsley leaves	125 mL
1-1/2 tsp	pine nuts or walnuts	7 mL
1	small clove garlic	1
Pinch	salt	Pinch
2 tbsp	olive oil	25 mL
2 tbsp	freshly grated Parmesan cheese	25 mL

- Spread cream cheese over 4 of the bread slices. Spread pesto over remaining bread slices, and sandwich on top of cream cheese.
- In shallow dish, beat eggs with milk. Dip both sides of sandwiches into egg mixture allowing bread to absorb mixture slightly.
- In skillet, heat vegetable oil over medium-high heat; cook sandwiches, in batches and adding more oil if necessary, for 1 to 2 minutes per side or until golden brown. Makes 4 servings.

- In food processor or blender, combine basil, pine nuts, garlic and salt; process until finely minced. With motor running, gradually add oil; process until mixture forms a paste. Stir in cheese. Makes 1/4 cup (50 mL).

TOMATO SALAD

Serve this quick little salad alongside French Toast with Pesto. In small bowl, combine 1 diced tomato, 1 tbsp (15 mL) wine vinegar and 1 tbsp (15 mL) olive oil. Season with salt and pepper to taste. Makes 4 small servings.

CRAB SALAD CROISSANTS WITH PEACHES AND PECANS

For a fashionably fast meal, luxurious crab (or lobster) salad is deliciously indulgent; for days when the budget won't stretch, chicken or salmon makes a great substitute. (photo, p. 33)

1 cup	cooked crabmeat, in small pieces	250 mL
1/4 cup	chopped green onion	50 mL
1/4 cup	chopped celery	50 mL
1	large peach	1
1/4 cup	pecan halves	50 mL
	Mayonnaise	
	Salt	

2	fresh croissants	2
	Leaf lettuce	
	Alfalfa sprouts	

- Combine crab, green onion and celery. Peel peach; cut half into slices and set aside for garnish. Dice remaining half and add to crab mixture along with half of the pecans. Add just enough mayonnaise to moisten. Season with salt to taste.
- Split croissants and fill with crab salad plus lettuce leaf. Garnish plate with alfalfa sprouts, reserved peach slices and pecans. Makes 2 servings.

Double-Olive Tuna Spread

DOUBLE-OLIVE TUNA SPREAD

This appetizer will keep for up to one week in the refrigerator. Serve as a spread with crackers or spoon into cherry tomatoes for a delicious appetizer.

1	can (6.5 oz/ 184 g) flaked white or light tuna, drained	1
1 cup	chopped fresh parsley	250 mL
1 cup	pitted black olives	250 mL
1/2 cup	pitted green olives	125 mL
1/4 cup	drained capers	50 mL
2 tbsp	lemon juice	25 mL
6	anchovy fillets	6
2 tsp	dried basil	10 mL
1	clove garlic	1
1/2 cup	olive oil	125 mL

• In food processor, combine tuna, parsley, black and green olives, capers, lemon juice, anchovy fillets, basil and garlic.
• With motor running, drizzle oil in thin steady stream through feed tube until mixture is smooth. Taste and adjust seasoning. Makes about 3 cups (750 mL).

TACOS WITH TOMATO AND CUCUMBER SALSA

If some family members dislike spicy tacos, reduce the amount of hot pepper flakes by half.

1 lb	ground beef	500 g
1	onion, chopped	1
2	gloves garlic, minced	2
1	can (7-1/2 oz/ 213 mL) tomato sauce	1
2 tsp	chili powder	10 mL
1 tsp	dried oregano	5 mL
1 tsp	cumin	5 mL
1/4 tsp	(approx) hot pepper flakes	1 mL
12	tacos (each 6 inches/15 cm)	12

TOPPINGS:

	Shredded lettuce	
	Chopped sweet green, red or yellow peppers	
	Chopped tomatoes	
	Grated part-skim cheese	
	Light sour cream or low-fat yogurt	
	Tomato and Cucumber Salsa (recipe follows)	

• In large skillet, cook beef over medium heat, breaking up with spoon, until brown, about 5 minutes. Pour off all fat. Add onion and garlic; cook until tender, about 3 minutes.

• Stir in tomato sauce, chili powder, oregano, cumin and hot pepper flakes; simmer for 5 to 10 minutes or until sauce-like consistency. Taste and add more hot pepper flakes if desired. If mixture becomes too dry, add a little water. Spoon into serving dish.

• **Toppings:** Place bowls of various toppings on table along with tacos.

• Let each person spoon some meat mixture into tacos, then add toppings of their choice. Makes 4 to 6 servings.

TOMATO AND CUCUMBER SALSA:

1	tomato, finely diced	1
1 cup	finely diced cucumber	250 mL
1	small green chili pepper (canned or fresh), chopped (or 1/4 tsp/1 mL hot pepper flakes)	1
2 tbsp	minced onion	25 mL
1 tbsp	chopped fresh coriander (optional)	15 mL
1 tbsp	wine vinegar	15 mL
Half	clove garlic, minced	Half

• In bowl, combine tomato, cucumber, chili pepper, onion, coriander (if using), vinegar and garlic. Transfer 1 cup (250 mL) to food processor or blender and purée; return to remaining mixture in bowl. Serve at room temperature or cover and refrigerate for up to 3 days if made more than a few hours in advance. Makes about 2 cups (500 mL).

If you use meat sauce sparingly and stay away from certain toppings, you can halve the fat and calorie content of tacos. Avocados are very high in fat and are best avoided. Olives are also high in fat and salt. You can use soft tortillas (which are lower in fat). Just crisp them in 400°F (200°C) oven for 10 minutes.

Tacos with Tomato and Cucumber Salsa

MUSHROOM AND MOZZARELLA PIZZA

You can glamorize these low-calorie pizzas by using wild mushrooms such as chanterelles, porcini and oyster. If the mushrooms are dried, first soak them in warm water until softened, about 15 minutes.

4	whole wheat pitas	4
3/4 lb	fresh mushrooms, thickly sliced	375 g
1/2 cup	water	125 mL
1-1/3 cups	2% cottage cheese (small curd)	325 mL
1/2 cup	shredded skim milk mozzarella cheese	125 mL
1 tsp	dried thyme	5 mL
1 tsp	dried oregano	5 mL
1 cup	tomato sauce	250 mL
2/3 cup	chopped fresh chives or parsley	150 mL

- Cut around edge of each pita to separate into two rounds; place on baking sheet. Broil for 1 to 2 minutes on each side or until crisp.
- In skillet, simmer mushrooms with water over medium heat, covered, for 5 minutes or until tender; drain.
- In bowl or food processor, combine cottage cheese, mozzarella cheese, thyme and oregano.
- Spread tomato sauce over pitas; top with cheese mixture. Spoon mushrooms over pitas and bake in 400°F (200°C) oven for 10 to 15 minutes or until heated through, cheese melts and sauce is bubbly. Sprinkle with chives. Makes 4 servings.

For Mushroom and Mozzarella Pizza, you can use individual whole wheat or plain pizza rounds instead of pitas.

PIZZA BREAD

Serve this with a Caesar salad for a hearty meal.

1/4 cup	butter or margarine, softened	50 mL
1	clove garlic, minced	1
1	loaf French bread, sliced in half lengthwise	1
1	can (7.5 oz/ 213 mL) tomato sauce	1
2 tbsp	tomato paste	25 mL
1 tsp	dried basil	5 mL
1 tsp	dried oregano	5 mL
1/2 lb	sliced salami or smoked meat, cut in strips	250 g
2 cups	shredded mozzarella cheese (about 1/2 lb/250 g)	500 mL
1/2 cup	freshly grated Parmesan cheese	125 mL

- Mix butter with garlic; spread over loaf halves.
- In bowl, mix together tomato sauce, tomato paste, basil and oregano; spread over buttered bread. Sprinkle evenly with salami, mozzarella and Parmesan.
- Place loaf halves on baking sheet; bake in 400°F (200°C) oven for 10 to 15 minutes or until cheeses melt. Cut into pieces and serve immediately. Makes 6 to 8 servings.

Muffuletta

MUFFULETTAS

The olive salad in this New Orleans specialty can also be used as part of an antipasto platter or puréed to make a delicious spread for crackers.

6	kaiser buns, split	6
12	very thin slices mortadella sausage	12
12	very thin slices prosciutto ham	12
12	very thin slices Genoa salami	12
12	thin slices provolone cheese	12
OLIVE SALAD:		
1 cup	pimiento-stuffed green olives	250 mL
1/2 cup	pitted black olives	125 mL
1/4 cup	good-quality olive oil	50 mL
1 tbsp	finely chopped pickled hot peppers	15 mL
1/2 tsp	dried oregano	2 mL
1/2 tsp	pepper	2 mL
2	cloves garlic, minced	2
2	anchovy fillets, minced	2

• **Olive Salad:** Chop green and black olives coarsely (or purée, if preferred). Combine with oil, hot peppers, oregano, pepper, garlic and anchovies.

• Spread cut surfaces of buns with any juices from olive salad. Place 2 slices each of mortadella, prosciutto and salami on bottom half of each bun; top with some of the salad. Place 2 slices of cheese on top of each; top with remaining buns. Press sandwich firmly together. Slice in half to serve. Makes 6 servings.

CROQUE-MONSIEUR

This tastes great when served with a mixed green salad garnished with cherry tomatoes. If there's room for dessert, make a quick apple crisp with canned applesauce.

2 tbsp	butter or margarine, softened	25 mL
1 tbsp	Dijon or prepared mustard	15 mL
12	slices firm white bread	12
1/2 lb	cooked ham, thinly sliced	250 g
1/4 cup	mayonnaise	50 mL
6 oz	Gruyère or Swiss cheese, shredded or thinly sliced	175 g
1/2 cup	water	125 mL
1/4 cup	all-purpose flour	50 mL
1 tsp	baking powder	5 mL
1/2 tsp	salt	2 mL
	Pepper	
3	eggs, lightly beaten	3
1/4 cup	butter	50 mL
2 tbsp	vegetable oil	25 mL

• Combine butter and mustard; spread over 6 bread slices. Top with ham slices.
• Spread mayonnaise over remaining bread slices and top with cheese. Press sandwich halves together.
• In shallow dish, mix together water, flour, baking powder, salt, and pepper to taste; blend in eggs, mixing well. Dip sandwiches into egg mixture, turning to coat both sides.
• In each of 2 large skillets, heat half of the butter and oil over medium-high heat until butter has melted. Brown sandwiches lightly on both sides. Cut each in half and serve on warm plates. Makes 6 servings.

VARIATIONS:

TONGUE CROQUE-MONSIEUR:
• Omit ham and substitute thin slices of cooked beef tongue.

CROQUE-MADAME:
• Omit ham and substitute cooked chicken or turkey slices; add thin slices of tomato, if desired.

MONTE CRISTO:
• Use only 1/4 lb (125 g) ham and add 1/4 lb (125 g) chicken slices.

LEAN BEEF SUPER SUPPER SANDWICHES

These tasty sandwiches have a crunchy sweet-and-hot topping. A simple lettuce and tomato salad is all that's needed for a quick supper.

1	small sweet red pepper	1
1	hot banana pepper	1
Half	Spanish onion	Half
2 tbsp	olive oil	25 mL
1	clove garlic, minced	1
2 tbsp	red wine	25 mL
4	minute steaks (4 oz/125 g each)	4
	Salt and pepper	
4	kaiser rolls	4
1/4 cup	crumbled blue cheese (optional)	50 mL

• Trim and seed red pepper; cut into 1/4-inch (5 mm) wide strips. Trim and seed banana pepper; cut into slivers. Halve onion lengthwise; cut into strips.
• In skillet, heat 1 tbsp (15 mL) of the oil over medium heat; add red and banana peppers, onion and garlic. Cook, stirring, for about 5 minutes or until onion is translucent. Add wine and cook, stirring, for 1 minute; transfer to bowl.
• Season steaks with salt and pepper to taste. Add remaining oil to pan and increase heat to medium-high; cook steaks for 2 minutes on each side or until browned.
• Meanwhile, halve rolls and place on baking sheet; broil until lightly toasted. Place each steak on roll; sprinkle with cheese (if using). Evenly spoon onion mixture over; top with remaining halves of rolls. Makes 4 servings.

Croque-Monsieur

AVOCADO MELTS

Avocado Melts

This open-faced, West Coast creation makes a substantial lunch or dinner.

6	whole wheat pita breads (each 5 in/ 12 cm)	6
1-1/2 cups	mashed ripe avocado	375 mL
1/4 cup	chopped green onion	50 mL
2 tbsp	lime or lemon juice	25 mL
2 tbsp	mayonnaise	25 mL
1/2 tsp	minced garlic	2 mL
1/2 tsp	salt	2 mL
Dash	hot pepper sauce	Dash
12	slices tomato (2 or 3 tomatoes)	12
3 cups	alfalfa sprouts	750 mL
2 cups	grated Monterey Jack cheese (about 1/2 lb/ 250 g)	500 mL

• Arrange pita breads on baking sheet.
• In bowl, combine avocado, green onion, lime juice, mayonnaise, garlic, salt and hot pepper sauce. Spread evenly over pitas and top with tomato slices, alfalfa sprouts and cheese. Bake in 400°F (200°C) oven for 5 to 7 minutes or until cheese melts. Serve immediately. Makes 6 servings.

OPEN-FACED HAMBURGERS

Spread this savory ground meat mixture on toast for a pleasant change from regular hamburgers. These "hamburgers" can be baked in a conventional or toaster oven. Serve with condiments such as mustard, relish, pickles, sliced tomatoes and lettuce. For dessert, serve sliced bananas sprinkled with brown sugar or drizzled lightly with maple syrup.

1/2 lb	lean ground beef	250 g
1/3 cup	chopped mushrooms	75 mL
2	green onions, chopped	2
1/2 tsp	salt	2 mL
1/2 tsp	dried basil	2 mL
	Pepper	
1/4 cup	sour cream	50 mL
4	slices French or whole wheat bread	4

• In bowl, mix together beef, mushrooms, onions, salt, basil, and pepper to taste; blend in sour cream.

• Toast bread slices. Spread each slice with beef mixture. In conventional or toaster oven, bake at 450°F (230°C) for about 10 minutes or until beef is cooked and top is evenly browned. Makes 4 servings.

Vary the flavor of Open-Faced Hamburgers with a change in toppings.
• **Top with Pesto (recipe, p. 38) spooned over thick tomato slices.**
• **Top with taco sauce, shredded lettuce and Monterey Jack cheese.**
• **Top with grainy German-style mustard and a spoonful of drained sauerkraut.**

OPEN-FACED STEAK SANDWICH WITH MUSHROOM SAUCE

You can substitute sirloin steak, cut into serving-sized pieces, if desired.

6 tbsp	butter	100 mL
4	boneless rib eye steaks, 3/4 in (2 cm) thick (1-1/2 lb/750 g total)	4
	Salt and pepper	
4	slices (1/2 in/1 cm thick) French bread	4
1/2 lb	mushrooms, halved if large	250 g
1/4 cup	dry sherry or beef stock	50 mL
1 tbsp	Dijon mustard	15 mL
1/3 cup	light or whipping cream	75 mL

• In skillet, melt half of the butter and brown steaks for 3 to 4 minutes on each side for medium-rare. Season with salt and pepper to taste; keep warm in 200°F (100°C) oven.

• Meanwhile, in separate skillet, melt remaining butter over medium heat and brown bread slices on both sides. Wrap in foil and keep warm in 200°F (100°C) oven.

• Add mushrooms to steak pan and cook until golden. Stir in sherry and mustard; cook for 1 minute. Stir in cream and cook for 2 minutes, stirring constantly.

• Remove bread from oven and place on warmed plates. Place steaks on top and spoon mushroom sauce over. Makes 4 servings.

Soups and Salads

Soup-and-salad suppers can be tasty alternatives to full-course dinners. They're practical, too, for those nights when every family member is going in a different direction. For a cosy winter meal, serve a hearty soup like Clam and Corn Chowder or Bean and Bacon Soup. Add an interesting bread and a salad for a complete help-yourself meal. In warmer weather, a chilled soup is the perfect opener. Choose from a variety of crisp salads, which can be quickly prepared as side dishes or even featured as one-plate suppers. For a delightfully different first course or light meal, combine a stir-fry of meat or fish with a hot dressing drizzled over torn greens like our Warm Steak Salad or Citrus Salmon Salad.

VEGETABLE CHILI CHOWDER

Your family will love this pleasantly spiced, hearty chili chowder.

1 tbsp	vegetable oil	15 mL
1	onion, chopped	1
1	sweet green pepper, diced	1
2	cloves garlic, minced	2
1 tbsp	chili powder	15 mL
1 tsp	ground cumin	5 mL
1	can (28 oz/796 mL) tomatoes (undrained), puréed	1
1	can (19 oz/ 540 mL) kidney beans, drained and rinsed	1
2	potatoes, diced	2
1 cup	corn kernels	250 mL
1 cup	chicken stock	250 mL
1/4 cup	finely chopped fresh parsley	50 mL
	Salt and pepper	

• In large saucepan, heat oil over medium-high heat; cook onion, green pepper and garlic for about 5 minutes or until softened. Add chili powder and cumin; cook, stirring, for 1 minute.

• Add tomatoes, kidney beans, potatoes, corn and chicken stock; bring to boil. Reduce heat and simmer for 15 to 20 minutes or until potatoes are tender and chowder has thickened. Stir in parsley; season with salt and pepper to taste. Makes 4 to 6 servings.

Vegetable Chili Chowder

BEAN AND BACON SOUP

For a quick family supper, make this tasty soup topped with bits of bacon. It's a combination of bean flavors that goes down smoothly on a winter night.

2 tbsp	unsalted butter	25 mL
1 cup	chopped onions	250 mL
3/4 cup	chopped celery	175 mL
3	cloves garlic, chopped	3
2-1/2 cups	chicken stock	625 mL
1-1/2 cups	frozen lima beans	375 mL
1 cup	frozen green beans, cut in 1-inch (2.5 cm) lengths	250 mL
	Salt and pepper	
6	slices back bacon, chopped (about 1/2 lb/250 g)	6

• In large heavy saucepan, melt butter over medium heat; cook onions and celery, stirring, for about 3 minutes or until vegetables are softened. Stir in garlic and cook for 1 minute or until fragrant.
• Add chicken stock and lima beans; bring to boil, reduce heat and simmer, covered, for 15 minutes. Transfer to blender or food processor and blend until smooth.
• Return mixture to saucepan; add green beans, and salt and pepper to taste. Heat gently for about 1 minute or until warmed through.
• Meanwhile, cook bacon until lightly browned. Ladle soup into bowls and sprinkle with bacon. Makes 4 servings.

If you are using canned or dried stocks instead of homemade, wait until the end of the cooking time before seasoning with salt.

TOMATO-BEAN CHOWDER

This hearty comforting soup is great for lunch on a cold winter day and light enough for a summer supper.

2 cups	beef or vegetable stock	500 mL
1	can (14 oz/398 mL) tomatoes (undrained)	1
2	onions, finely chopped	2
Half	sweet green pepper, chopped	Half
1 tsp	chili powder	5 mL
1	can (19 oz/540 mL) red kidney beans, drained	1
	Salt and pepper	
GARNISH:		
1/2 cup	finely chopped fresh parsley	125 mL

• In large heavy saucepan, combine stock, tomatoes, onions, green pepper and chili powder; bring to boil, reduce heat and simmer for 15 minutes, breaking up tomatoes with back of spoon.
• Add kidney beans; simmer for 10 minutes and season with salt and pepper to taste. Garnish with parsley. Makes about 4 to 6 servings.

If you prefer to use dried beans, follow these easy directions.

To quick soak 1 cup (250 mL) dried beans: Rinse and sort beans before soaking, discarding blemished beans. Cover dried beans with 3 cups (750 mL) cold water; bring to boil. Boil gently for 2 minutes. Remove from heat; cover and let stand for 1 hour. Drain and cook.

To cook dried beans after soaking: In heavy saucepan, cover drained soaked beans with 2-1/2 cups (625 mL) fresh water and 1 tbsp (15 mL) vegetable oil. Bring to boil; reduce heat and simmer, covered, for 1 to 2 hours (depending on type of bean) or until tender. Drain.

Note: 1 cup (250 mL) dried beans yields 2 cups (500 mL) cooked.

*Hearty Ham and
Vegetable Bean Soup*

HEARTY HAM AND VEGETABLE BEAN SOUP

Having this soup on hand means anyone at home can get a quick meal at a moment's notice. It can be stored, covered, in the refrigerator for up to four days.

1 cup	uncooked pasta	250 mL
1 tbsp	vegetable oil	15 mL
2	onions, chopped	2
4 cups	chicken stock	1 L
2	carrots, chopped	2
2	cloves garlic, minced	2
1	sweet red or green pepper, chopped	1
1	small zucchini, chopped	1
1	can (28 oz/ 796 mL) plum tomatoes	1
2-1/2 cups	cubed cooked trimmed ham steak	625 mL
1	can (19 oz/540 mL) red kidney beans, drained	1
1	can (19 oz/540 mL) chick-peas or black-eyed peas, drained	1
4 cups	spinach leaves, chopped	1 L
1 tsp	dried thyme	5 mL
1/2 tsp	dried savory	2 mL
1/2 tsp	dried basil or oregano	2 mL
1/4 tsp	pepper	1 mL
	Salt	

• In large pot of boiling water, cook pasta until al dente (tender but firm); drain and rinse under cold water.

• In large Dutch oven, heat oil over medium heat; cook onions, stirring, until softened, 3 to 5 minutes. Add stock, carrots, garlic, sweet pepper and zucchini; bring to simmer and cook for 3 to 5 minutes or until vegetables are tender.

• Stir in pasta, tomatoes, ham, beans, chick-peas, spinach, thyme, savory, basil, pepper, and salt to taste. Simmer for 5 minutes. Makes about 8 servings.

CLAM AND CORN CHOWDER

On a cold winter night, this hearty, chunky-style soup fills the bill. To save time, cook the bacon while you prepare the potatoes. Serve with thick slices of crusty bread. A baked apple, cooked in the microwave oven, makes a quick and tasty dessert.

4	strips bacon	4
1	onion, chopped	1
1	can (5 oz/142 g) clams	1
2 cups	diced peeled potatoes	500 mL
1-1/2 cups	milk	375 mL
	Salt and pepper	
1	can (19 oz/ 540 mL) cream-style corn	1

• In heavy saucepan, cook bacon over medium-high heat until crisp, about 5 minutes. Pour off all but 1 tbsp (15 mL) drippings. Drain bacon on paper towels and cut into 1/2-inch (1 cm) pieces.
• Add onion to drippings; cook for 2 minutes or until softened but not browned. Drain clams, reserving juice; set clams aside. Stir clam juice and potatoes into saucepan; cook for 5 minutes or until potatoes are tender.
• Blend in milk, and salt and pepper to taste. Add corn and clams. Heat through and serve, sprinkled with bacon. Makes about 4 servings.

VARIATION:

SALMON AND CORN CHOWDER:
• Substitute 1 can (7.5 oz/213 mL) salmon for the clams. Drain salmon, adding water or chicken stock to make 2/3 cup (150 mL) liquid to use instead of drained clam juice. Remove salmon bones and skin, if desired. Proceed as above.

CURRIED CAULIFLOWER AND TOFU SOUP

Tofu makes this flavorful vegetable soup a main-course dish. Prepare the vegetables while the tofu drains.

1/2 lb	tofu	250 g
1	cauliflower	1
1/4 cup	butter	50 mL
2	onions, chopped	2
2	cloves garlic, minced	2
3	carrots, finely diced	3
2	potatoes, finely diced	2
2 tsp	each ground cumin, coriander and curry powder	10 mL
5 cups	chicken stock	1.25 L
1 tsp	salt	5 mL
1 cup	peas (fresh or frozen)	250 mL
1/4 cup	chopped fresh parsley	50 mL

• Drain tofu; place between triple thickness of paper towels on board. Top with baking sheet weighed down with cans of food. Let drain for 20 minutes. Cut into 1/2-inch (1 cm) cubes; set aside. Cut cauliflower into small florets; set aside.
• In large saucepan, melt butter over medium heat; sauté cauliflower, onions, garlic, carrots and potatoes for 5 minutes.
• Stir in cumin, coriander and curry powder; cook, stirring, for 1 minute. Stir in stock and salt; bring to boil. Reduce heat and simmer, covered, until vegetables are tender, about 8 minutes.
• Stir in tofu and peas; simmer for 1 to 2 minutes or until peas are heated through. Taste and adjust seasoning if necessary. Serve garnished with parsley. Makes 6 servings.

MUSHROOM CONSOMMÉ

A little butter adds flavor and substance to this easy-to-make soup. In saucepan, melt 1 tbsp (15 mL) butter over medium heat; stir in 2 cups (500 mL) sliced mushrooms (about 1/4 lb/125 g) and cook, covered, for 2 to 3 minutes or until mushrooms release their juices. Add 3 cups (750 mL) chicken stock and bring to simmer; cook for 5 minutes. Stir in 2 tbsp (25 mL) dry sherry; season with salt and pepper to taste. Makes 4 servings.

Curried Cauliflower and Tofu Soup

CREAM OF VEGETABLE SOUP

A hint of curry perks up this soup's flavor. Use frozen vegetables or left-over cooked ones.

2 tbsp	butter	25 mL
1	onion, coarsely chopped	1
2 tbsp	all-purpose flour	25 mL
2 cups	chicken stock	500 mL
1-1/2 cups	frozen mixed vegetables	375 mL
1/2 tsp	curry powder	2 mL
Pinch	nutmeg	Pinch
3/4 cup	milk	175 mL
	Salt and pepper	

• In saucepan, melt butter over medium heat; add onion and cook for about 5 minutes or until softened and translucent. Remove from heat and stir in flour; gradually blend in stock. Return to heat and cook, stirring, until thickened.
• Add vegetables, curry powder and nutmeg; cover and cook over medium-low heat for 10 minutes. Gradually stir in milk and cook, stirring constantly, just until heated through, about 5 minutes. Season with salt and pepper to taste. Makes 4 servings.

VARIATION:

CREAM OF CARROT SOUP:
• Substitute 1-1/2 cups (375 mL) frozen sliced carrots for the mixed vegetables.

CURRIED SQUASH SOUP

Enjoy the subtle flavors and smooth consistency of this colorful soup on a cold winter evening. (photo, p. 70)

2 tbsp	butter	25 mL
1	large onion, chopped	1
1 tbsp	all-purpose flour	15 mL
2 cups	chicken stock	500 mL
1	pkg (400 g) frozen cooked squash, thawed	1
1	small apple, peeled and diced	1
1 tsp	curry powder	5 mL
1/4 tsp	ground coriander	1 mL
3/4 cup	milk	175 mL
	Salt and pepper	
	Plain yogurt	

• In saucepan, melt butter over medium heat; cook onion for 4 minutes or until tender. Stir in flour; gradually stir in stock. Add squash, apple, curry powder and coriander; bring to boil. Reduce heat and simmer, covered, for 10 minutes.

• Transfer to food processor or blender; purée until smooth. Return to saucepan. Stir in milk and cook, stirring, until heated through. Season with salt and pepper to taste. Ladle into soup bowls; garnish with dollop of yogurt and swirl with knife tip. Makes about 4 servings.

BROCCOLI AND RED ONION SOUP

This quick and easy-to-make soup has a wonderful flavor without high calories. Garnish with red onion slices and dill, if desired.

2 tbsp	butter or vegetable oil	25 mL
1	red onion, finely chopped	1
1	clove garlic, minced	1
1	small bunch broccoli (1 lb/ 500 g)	1
3 cups	chicken stock	750 mL
1	potato, peeled and diced	1
1/4 cup	chopped fresh dill or parsley	50 mL
	Salt and pepper	

Broccoli and Red Onion Soup

• In large saucepan or Dutch oven, melt butter; add onion and garlic and cook until tender and fragrant.

• Meanwhile, trim broccoli, discarding coarse ends. Cut florets into 2-inch (5 cm) pieces and slice stalks thinly. Add to onion mixture in saucepan.

• Stir in stock and potato. Bring to boil; reduce heat and cook, covered, for 10 minutes. Stir in dill and season with salt and pepper to taste. Cook for about 10 minutes longer or until vegetables are tender.

• In blender, food processor or by pushing through food mill, purée soup. Taste and adjust seasoning, if necessary. Reheat soup, if necessary. Makes 6 servings.

EIGHT TREASURE SOUP

This is a quick but delicious variation of the classic Chinese soup that is served on special occasions.

3 cups	chicken stock	750 mL
1 tsp	teriyaki sauce	5 mL
1 cup	bean sprouts	250 mL
1/2 cup	thinly sliced mushrooms	125 mL
1/2 cup	snow peas, trimmed (or 1/2 cup/125 mL frozen peas)	125 mL
4	small green onions, cut in 1-inch (2.5 cm) lengths	4
1 lb	tofu square (about 3 inches/ 7 cm), drained and cubed	500 g
	Salt and pepper	

• In saucepan, bring stock and teriyaki sauce to simmer. Add bean sprouts, mushrooms, snow peas and onions; cook for 5 minutes.
• Add tofu cubes; cook just until tofu is heated through, 2 to 3 minutes. Season with salt and pepper to taste. Makes 4 servings.

SPICY CLAMATO BISQUE

Here's a zippy starter for any luncheon or dinner. Increase the spiciness by adding hot pepper sauce to taste.

1-1/2 cups	beef stock	375 mL
1-1/2 cups	tomato juice	375 mL
1	can (5 oz/142 g) baby clams (undrained)	1
1 tsp	lemon juice	5 mL
1 tsp	Worcestershire sauce	5 mL
1/2 tsp	curry powder	2 mL
1/2 tsp	salt	2 mL
1/4 cup	dry sherry	50 mL

• In saucepan, combine stock, tomato juice, clams, lemon juice, Worcestershire, curry powder and salt; bring to boil. Remove from heat; stir in sherry. Serve immediately. Makes 4 servings.

CHILLED CUCUMBER SOUP

This refreshing starter takes 5 minutes to make. If you want to speed up the chilling, pour soup into cups, add an ice cube to each and place in freezer for about 20 minutes.

4	green onions (white parts plus about half of green)	4
1	clove garlic	1
2 tbsp	fresh dill or parsley (or 2 tsp/ 10 mL dried)	25 mL
2	cucumbers, peeled, seeded and cut in chunks	2
2 cups	buttermilk	500 mL
1 cup	full-flavored chicken stock (or 1 10-oz/284 mL can chicken broth, undiluted)	250 mL
	Salt and pepper	

• In food processor, process onions, garlic and dill until finely chopped. Add cucumbers; process until finely chopped. Turn chopped mixture into bowl. Stir in buttermilk and chicken stock. Season with salt and pepper to taste. Chill until very cold. Serve in chilled soup cups. Makes about 6 servings.

TOFU TIPS

The most commonly available tofu is the regular grade. Rectangular 1-pound (500 g) cakes are water-packed in sealed plastic cartons and are found in the produce sections of most supermarkets. Look for the "best before" on the carton and remember, the fresher the better.

Storing: Tofu must always be covered with fresh water to prevent a thick skin from forming. Change the water daily and store the tofu in the refrigerator.

ARTICHOKE SALAD IN ROMAINE BOATS

Artichoke Salad in Romaine Boats

Choose well-curved, inner leaves of romaine to hold this hearty salad.

1	can (14 oz/398 mL) artichoke hearts, well drained	1
Half	sweet red or yellow pepper	Half
1/4 cup	pitted black olives, halved	50 mL
2 tbsp	chopped fresh parsley	25 mL
2 tbsp	vegetable oil	25 mL
1 tbsp	wine vinegar	15 mL
1/2 tsp	Dijon mustard	2 mL
	Salt and pepper	
4	inner leaves romaine lettuce	4

• Quarter artichokes. Cut sweet pepper into 1-inch (2.5 cm) squares. In bowl, combine artichokes, sweet pepper and olives; add parsley and toss lightly to mix.
• In small screw-top jar, combine oil, vinegar, mustard, and salt and pepper to taste; shake well. Pour over artichoke mixture and toss lightly. Serve in lettuce leaves. Makes 4 servings.

CARROT, CELERY AND PECAN SALAD

Colorful, crunchy and mildly sweet, this is good to serve as a side salad with sandwiches or cold cuts. Walnuts or almonds may be used instead of pecans.

4	carrots, coarsely grated	4
1	stalk celery, very thinly sliced	1
1/2 cup	pecan halves	125 mL
1/4 cup	sour cream	50 mL
2 tbsp	mayonnaise	25 mL
1 tbsp	peach or mango chutney	15 mL
1 tsp	lemon juice	5 mL
	Salt and pepper	

• In bowl, toss together carrots, celery and pecans.
• Combine sour cream, mayonnaise, chutney and lemon juice; season with salt and pepper to taste. Pour over carrot mixture; toss to coat. Taste and adjust seasoning. Serve immediately or cover and refrigerate for up to 10 hours. Makes 4 servings.

CURLY ENDIVE WITH WALNUTS AND BLUE CHEESE

The mild tender hearts of either curly endive or escarole blend particularly well with crunchy walnuts and a nippy blue cheese. Serve this for lunch or supper with a hearty soup or an egg dish such as an omelette or frittata.

2	heads curly endive (each 3/4 lb/375 g)	2
1/2 cup	chopped walnuts	125 mL
1/2 cup	crumbled blue cheese (2 oz/ 60 g)	125 mL
DRESSING:		
1/3 cup	olive oil	75 mL
2 tbsp	white wine vinegar	25 mL
1 tbsp	walnut oil (optional)	15 mL
1 tsp	Dijon mustard	5 mL
1/2 tsp	salt	2 mL
Pinch	pepper	Pinch

• Remove and discard outer leaves from endive; break curly creamy yellow or light green leaves into bite-sized pieces. Place in shallow salad bowl; sprinkle with walnuts and cheese.
• **Dressing:** In jar with tight-fitting lid, shake together olive oil, vinegar, walnut oil (if using), mustard, salt and pepper; taste and adjust seasoning if necessary. Drizzle over salad; toss to mix. Makes 6 to 8 servings.

HEARTS OF ROMAINE AND CUCUMBER SALAD

Any type of lettuce or mixed greens can be substituted for the romaine.

1	head romaine lettuce, outer leaves removed	1
1	small cucumber (or half English cucumber), thinly sliced	1
YOGURT-GARLIC DRESSING:		
1/2 cup	plain yogurt	125 mL
1 tbsp	vegetable oil	15 mL
2	cloves garlic, minced	2
	Salt and pepper	

• Tear lettuce into bite-sized pieces. Place in salad bowl along with cucumber.
• **Yogurt-Garlic Dressing:** Mix together yogurt, oil and garlic; season with salt and pepper to taste. Pour over lettuce mixture and toss lightly. Makes 4 servings.

HOT CRAB AND AVOCADO SALAD

The slightly bitter taste of radicchio adds an interesting flavor to this colorful warm salad. You can substitute frozen crabmeat or shrimp for the canned crab.

1	head Bibb lettuce	1
1	small head radicchio	1
1	bunch watercress	1
1/3 cup	vegetable oil	75 mL
1/4 cup	lemon juice	50 mL
2 tsp	grated gingerroot	10 mL
1/2 tsp	dry mustard	2 mL
1/2 tsp	salt	2 mL
Pinch	pepper	Pinch
1	can (6 oz/170 g) crabmeat, drained and flaked	1
1	large avocado, peeled and cubed	1
2	green oinions, thinly sliced	2

• Tear Bibb lettuce and radicchio into bite-sized pieces; divide among 4 plates. Arrange watercress on top; set aside.
• In saucepan, combine oil, lemon juice, gingerroot, mustard, salt and pepper; bring to boil, stirring constantly.
• Add crabmeat, avocado and onions; reduce heat and cook, stirring constantly, for 1 to 2 minutes or until warmed through. Spoon over greens. Serve immediately. Makes 4 servings.

CUCUMBER SALAD WITH YOGURT AND DILL

This refreshing summer salad takes only a few minutes to prepare. If desired, make it in the morning and refrigerate to blend the flavors.

1	seedless cucumber, peeled and thinly sliced	1
	Salt	
1 cup	plain yogurt	250 mL
2 tbsp	chopped fresh dill	25 mL
1 tsp	lemon juice	5 mL

• In colander, arrange cucumber slices in layers, lightly salting each layer to draw out moisture. Let stand for 10 minutes; rinse with cold water and pat dry. Place in small salad bowl.
• Mix together yogurt, dill and lemon juice. Add to cucumbers, tossing lightly to mix. Serve at room temperature or slightly chilled. Makes 4 servings.

WARM PASTA SEAFOOD SALAD

Warm seafood salads have been in vogue for a few years; here's one that calls for pasta, and the mix is sensational. The combined Oriental-Italian influence reflects a popular pairing of styles. (photo, p. 33)

4 cups	mixed torn salad greens	1 L
2	heads Belgian endive, separated in leaves	2
4 cups	shelled seafood, whole or in pieces*	1 L
1/2 lb	Oriental noodles**	250 g
	Salt and pepper	

DRESSING:

1/2 cup	vegetable oil	125 mL
1/4 cup	olive oil	50 mL
1/4 cup	rice vinegar	50 mL
1 tbsp	lime or lemon juice	15 mL
1	green onion, chopped	1
1 tbsp	minced fresh parsley	15 mL
1 tsp	dried *herbes de Provence* (or 1 tbsp/15 mL chopped fresh mixed herbs)	5 mL
1	small clove garlic, minced	1
1/2 tsp	salt	2 mL
	Pepper	

For the mixed torn salad greens in Warm Pasta Seafood Salad you can use a combination of mâche, arugula, watercress and spinach. Garnish the finished salad with sweet peas or edible flowers if you like.

• **Dressing:** In small saucepan, combine vegetable and olive oils, vinegar, lime juice, onion, parsley, *herbes de Provence*, garlic, salt, and pepper to taste. Heat just until warm to the touch; keep warm over low heat (or use microwave oven to warm dressing quickly as needed).

• In centres of 4 individual serving plates, arrange mixed greens; arrange leaves of endive around edge. Set aside.

• In saucepan of boiling salted water, cook seafood just until tender; drain. Cut any large pieces into bite-sized pieces. Toss with small amount of warm dressing just to moisten; set aside at room temperature.

• In large pot of boiling salted water, cook noodles just until tender but firm; drain thoroughly. Toss with about 1/4 cup (50 mL) warm dressing. Season with salt and pepper to taste.

• Immediately arrange warm pasta on top of greens. Top with seafood. Drizzle with a little more dressing. Makes 4 servings.

*Lobster, crab, shrimp, scallops, mussels, squid, salmon, firm white fish. You will need only about 1 lb (500 g) shelled seafood, less if you use a small amount of one or two varieties of shellfish and combine it with other fish.

**Available in specialty shops and some supermarkets (or substitute Italian pasta such as angel hair or fine egg noodles).

BROCCOLI SALAD WITH SUNFLOWER SEEDS

For full flavor, serve this salad at room temperature.

1 lb	broccoli	500 g
2 tbsp	chopped red onion	25 mL
2 tbsp	sunflower seeds	25 mL
2 tbsp	olive oil	25 mL
1 tbsp	lemon juice	15 mL
	Salt and pepper	

• Peel and slice broccoli stalks; cut tops into florets about 2 inches (5 cm) long. In boiling water, blanch for 3 to 4 minutes or until tender-crisp; drain and rinse under cold running water and drain again.

• In serving bowl, toss together broccoli, onion, sunflower seeds, oil, lemon juice, and salt and pepper to taste. Makes about 4 servings.

CITRUS SALMON SALAD

Served with warm crusty bread or croissants, this light and easy salad makes a perfect luncheon or supper menu. For heartier appetites, start with a bowl of soup. The recipe can be easily doubled to serve four.

1	can (7.5 oz/ 213 g) salmon, drained	1
3/4 cup	chopped celery	175 mL
2 tbsp	chopped green onion	25 mL
1	each grapefruit and orange, peeled and sectioned	1
1/4 cup	vegetable oil	50 mL
1 tbsp	cider vinegar	15 mL
1 tbsp	tomato ketchup	15 mL
Pinch	each dry mustard, salt and pepper	Pinch
	Bibb lettuce	
	Watercress (optional)	

• In bowl, flake salmon; add celery and onion. Drain grapefruit and orange sections; add to salmon mixture.
• In small bowl or measuring cup, combine oil, vinegar, ketchup, mustard, salt and pepper; mix well and pour over salmon mixture. Toss gently to mix.
• Arrange Bibb lettuce cups on 2 salad plates. Spoon salmon mixture evenly into cups. Garnish with watercress (if using) and serve immediately. Makes 2 servings.

Choosing salad greens for a warm salad: Mix and match bitter greens such as arugula, curly endive, radicchio, escarole, dandelions and watercress along with more tender, mild greens such as Boston, leaf, lamb or oak lettuce and spinach. Bitter greens are sturdy and will not wilt as quickly when tossed with a hot dressing. They add crunch as well.

SKILLET CHICKEN SALAD

For a real change of pace from regular cold salads, try this colorful hot salad—it's just the answer for a light supper.

4	boneless skinless chicken breasts (about 1 lb/ 500 g)	4
1	sweet red pepper	1
Half	bunch broccoli (about 1/2 lb/ 250 g)	Half
1/4 cup	vegetable oil	50 mL
1/4 cup	chicken stock	50 mL
3 tbsp	vinegar	50 mL
1 tbsp	Dijon mustard	15 mL
1 tsp	dried tarragon	5 mL
	Salt and pepper	
1 cup	tiny whole mushrooms	250 mL
2	green onions, chopped	2
	Boston or leaf lettuce	

• Cut chicken crosswise into 1/2-inch (1 cm) wide strips. Seed and core red pepper; cut into strips. Cut broccoli into small florets; peel and cut stems into 1/4-inch (5 mm) thick slices.
• In large skillet, heat 2 tbsp (25 mL) of the oil over medium heat; cook chicken, stirring, for about 4 minutes or until golden outside and no longer pink inside. Using slotted spoon, transfer chicken to warmed bowl; cover and keep warm.
• In same skillet, heat remaining oil; cook red pepper and broccoli for 2 minutes. Stir in stock and reduce heat to low; cover and steam for 2 minutes. Using slotted spoon, add red pepper and broccoli to chicken.
• In same skillet, bring vinegar to boil, scraping up brown bits on bottom of pan. Stir in mustard, tarragon, and salt and pepper to taste. Stir in mushrooms and onions. Return chicken mixture and any juices that have accumulated in bowl to skillet. Cook for a few seconds or until heated through.
• Line 4 dinner plates with lettuce; top with salad. Makes 4 servings.

Warm Mexican Salad

WARM MEXICAN SALAD

All the flavors of a taco in a dish! Complete the meal with melon wedges sprinkled with lime juice.

3/4 lb	lean ground beef	375 g
1	small onion, chopped	1
2/3 cup	taco sauce (mild or hot)	150 mL
1/2 tsp	salt	2 mL
1/2 tsp	chili powder	2 mL
1/4 tsp	cumin	1 mL
1/2 cup	sour cream	125 mL
2 cups	shredded lettuce	500 mL
1-1/2 cups	crumbled tortillas or corn chips	375 mL
1 cup	shredded Monterey Jack or mild Cheddar cheese	250 mL
1	small avocado (optional)	1
1/4 cup	sliced pitted black olives (optional)	50 mL

• In skillet, brown beef and onion over medium-high heat, stirring to break up. Drain off excess fat. Blend in taco sauce, salt, chili powder and cumin. Reduce heat to medium-low; stir for about 5 minutes or until heated through. Taste and adjust seasoning. Stir in sour cream.

• Toss with lettuce, tortillas and cheese. Peel, pit and chop avocado (if using); add to mixture, along with olives (if using), or arrange as in our photograph. Makes 4 servings.

• **Microwave Directions:** Crumble beef into 8-cup (2 L) microwaveable bowl; add onion. Microwave at High for 3 to 5 minutes or until meat is no longer pink and onion is tender, stirring once; stir and drain. Mix in taco sauce, salt, chili powder and cumin. Microwave at Medium (50%) for 3 minutes or until heated through, stirring once partway through cooking. Proceed as above.

ORANGE, OLIVE AND ONION SALAD

This salad can be attractively arranged on individual salad plates or tossed together in a large bowl with just enough dressing to coat lettuce. If available, substitute one bunch of arugula, mâche or watercress for one of the heads of Boston lettuce.

2	small heads Boston, leaf or romaine lettuce	2
2	oranges	2
Half	red onion, thinly sliced	Half
1/3 cup	black olives, halved and pitted	75 mL

DRESSING:

2 tbsp	white wine vinegar	25 mL
1/2 tsp	dried basil	2 mL
1/2 tsp	granulated sugar	2 mL
1/2 tsp	Dijon mustard	2 mL
1/2 cup	vegetable oil	125 mL
	Salt and pepper	

• Tear lettuce leaves into bite-sized pieces. Slice tops and bottoms from oranges; cut away rind, removing all white pith. Cut oranges into thin rounds. Separate onion slices into rings.
• **Dressing:** In food processor or bowl, combine vinegar, basil, sugar and mustard. With motor running or whisking constantly, gradually pour in oil until blended. Season with salt and pepper to taste.
• On individual salad plates, arrange row of orange slices; place olive in centre of each slice. Place lettuce beside orange slices; top with onion rings. Drizzle dressing over lettuce. Makes 6 to 8 servings.

ROMAINE SALAD WITH CAESAR DRESSING

This blender dressing gives you Caesar flavor in a hurry. It's equally good on romaine or spinach, or a combination of both. Any leftover dressing may be stored in the refrigerator for up to 2 days.

2	heads romaine lettuce	2
	Freshly grated Parmesan cheese	
	Croutons (optional)	

DRESSING:

1	egg (or 2 yolks)	1
2	cloves garlic	2
3 tbsp	red wine vinegar	50 mL
1 tbsp	lemon juice	15 mL
2 tsp	Dijon mustard	10 mL
1/2 tsp	salt	2 mL
1/4 tsp	pepper	1 mL
1/4 tsp	Worcestershire sauce	1 mL
1/4 cup	freshly grated Parmesan cheese	50 mL
1 cup	olive oil	250 mL

• **Dressing:** In blender, combine egg, garlic, vinegar, lemon juice, mustard, salt, pepper, Worcestershire sauce and Parmesan; process for a few seconds to combine. With machine running, gradually add oil in steady stream. Taste and adjust seasoning if necessary.
• Tear romaine into salad bowl. Toss with enough dressing to moisten. Add additional Parmesan to taste; toss again. Sprinkle with croutons (if using). Makes about 8 servings.

COLESLAW

Here's a simple recipe for a basic coleslaw. It will keep for several days, covered, in the refrigerator. For variations, see sidebar this page.

2 cups	finely sliced (or coarsely shredded) cabbage	500 mL
1	large carrot, grated	1
1/4 cup	(approx) mayonnaise	50 mL
	Salt and pepper	

• In salad bowl, mix cabbage, carrot and mayonnaise. Add salt and pepper to taste, and more mayonnaise, if necessary, to moisten. Makes 4 servings.

COLESLAW VARIATIONS

For extra flavor, add one or two of the following to the basic coleslaw recipe:
• 1 chopped apple
• 1 chopped green onion
• 1/4 cup (50 mL) chopped fresh parsley
• 1/4 cup (50 mL) raisins
• 1/2 cup (125 mL) bean sprouts
• 1 tbsp (15 mL) finely chopped fresh chives
• 1/2 tsp (2 mL) caraway seeds
• 1 tbsp (15 mL) chopped fresh dill
• 1/2 cup (125 mL) chopped celery or sweet red or green pepper

Warm Bacon and Egg Salad

WARM BACON AND EGG SALAD

This warm salad makes a perfect brunch dish. Follow it with fresh fruit and coffee cake.

1/2 cup	olive oil	125 mL
1	clove garlic, minced	1
12	slices French bread	12
8	slices bacon	8
1/3 cup	wine vinegar	75 mL
1 tbsp	minced shallot	15 mL
4	eggs	4
6 cups	torn mixed greens	1.5 L
1/4 tsp	salt	1 mL
Pinch	pepper	Pinch

• Mix together 2 tbsp (25 mL) of the oil with garlic; brush lightly all over bread slices. Arrange on baking sheet and broil each side until golden brown; set aside.

• In skillet, cook bacon over medium heat until crisp, about 5 minutes. Let cool slightly and crumble; set aside. Pour off fat from skillet. To skillet, add vinegar and shallot; cook over medium-high heat, scraping up brown bits, for about 2 minutes or until liquid is reduced by half.

• Meanwhile, in separate skillet, poach eggs.

• In bowl, toss greens with remaining oil; pour hot dressing over and sprinkle with salt and pepper. Toss well and arrange on salad plates. Slip poached egg onto each salad; sprinkle with bacon and surround with toast. Makes 4 servings.

WARM STEAK SALAD

Warm Steak Salad

Start the summer salad season with an easy fresh-tasting warm steak salad. Next time try one of the variations (sidebar opposite page) and enjoy sizzling new tastes and textures.

2	cloves garlic	2
1/2 cup	olive oil	125 mL
1 tsp	Dijon mustard	5 mL
6 cups	torn salad greens	1.5 L
12	thin slices French stick (baguette)	12
1/4 cup	vegetable oil	50 mL
1/2 lb	sirloin steak, thinly sliced	250 g
1/3 cup	red wine vinegar	75 mL
1	sweet red pepper, thinly sliced	1
2 tbsp	chopped shallots	25 mL
1 tsp	dried thyme	5 mL
	Salt and pepper	

• Mince 1 of the garlic cloves. In salad bowl, combine minced garlic, 1/3 cup (75 mL) of the olive oil and mustard; add greens and toss. Set aside.

• Halve remaining garlic clove and rub over bread slices. In large skillet, heat vegetable oil over medium heat; cook bread, turning once, for 3 to 5 minutes or until crisp and golden brown. Drain croûtes on paper towels and set aside.

• In same skillet, heat remaining olive oil over medium-high heat; cook steak, stirring, for 2 to 3 minutes or until lightly browned but still pink inside. Using slotted spoon, transfer to salad bowl.

• To skillet, add vinegar, red pepper, shallots and thyme; cook over medium-high heat, scraping up brown bits, for 2 to 3 minutes or until liquid is reduced by half. Immediately pour over salad and toss well. Season with salt and pepper to taste.

• Arrange croûtes around salad and serve immediately. Makes 4 servings.

MEDITERRANEAN SALAD

Enjoy this simple Greek-style salad when the summer garden is at its best. The ingredients can be varied according to availability and preference, and can also be combined with salad greens if you like.

5	ripe tomatoes	5
2	cucumbers, peeled and seeded	2
1	small sweet red or green pepper (optional)	1
2 oz	feta cheese, cut in small cubes	60 g
1/2 cup	black olives	125 mL
DRESSING:		
2 tbsp	red wine vinegar	25 mL
1 tbsp	lemon juice	15 mL
1	clove garlic, minced	1
1 tsp	salt	5 mL
1/2 tsp	pepper	2 mL
2/3 cup	olive oil	150 mL
4	green onions, chopped	4
1/4 cup	chopped fresh basil	50 mL

• Cut tomatoes, cucumbers, and red pepper (if using) into small chunks. Combine in salad bowl with feta and olives.
• **Dressing:** Whisk together vinegar, lemon juice, garlic, salt and pepper. Gradually whisk in olive oil. Stir in green onions and basil. Pour over salad and toss gently. Makes about 6 servings.

SPINACH AND ROMAINE SALAD WITH HORSERADISH DRESSING

Add zing to a simple green salad with this zesty horseradish dressing.

1	pkg (10 oz/284 g) spinach, trimmed	1
Half	head romaine lettuce	Half
HORSERADISH DRESSING:		
3 tbsp	sour cream	50 mL
4 tsp	drained prepared horseradish	20 mL
1 tbsp	white vinegar	15 mL
1 tsp	Dijon mustard	5 mL
3 tbsp	vegetable oil	50 mL

• **Horseradish Dressing:** In small bowl, whisk together sour cream, horseradish, vinegar and mustard; gradually pour in oil, whisking constantly.
• Tear spinach and lettuce into bite-sized pieces; place in salad bowl and toss with dressing. Makes about 4 servings.

AVOCADO AND WALNUT SALAD

Avocados or walnuts dress up any dish but combining the two makes an especially chic salad. Be sure to use only fresh walnuts.

1	head Boston lettuce, separated	1
1	large ripe avocado	1
1/4 cup	chopped walnuts	50 mL
DRESSING:		
1/2 cup	vegetable oil	125 mL
2 tbsp	white wine vinegar	25 mL
1 tsp	Dijon mustard	5 mL
Pinch	dried tarragon	Pinch
	Salt and pepper	

• Arrange lettuce leaves on 3 or 4 individual salad plates. Peel and pit avocado; slice thinly lengthwise and arrange on lettuce. Sprinkle with nuts.
• **Dressing:** In small jar or bowl, combine oil, vinegar, mustard, tarragon, and salt and pepper to taste. Drizzle over salads. Serve at room temperature within 30 minutes. Makes 3 or 4 servings.

Try these variations to the Warm Steak Salad.

Warm Breast of Chicken Salad: Substitute thinly sliced chicken breast for the beef. Cook chicken, stirring, for 3 to 4 minutes or until no longer pink inside. Substitute 1/4 cup (50 mL) tarragon vinegar and 2 tbsp (25 mL) lemon juice for red wine vinegar. Use dried tarragon instead of thyme.

Warm Calves' Liver Salad: Substitute thinly sliced calves' liver for the beef. Cook liver, stirring, for 2 to 3 minutes or until lightly browned but still slightly pink inside. Use balsamic vinegar instead of red wine vinegar.

Warm Scallop Salad: Substitute scallops for beef; cook, stirring, for 3 to 4 minutes or just until opaque. Substitute 1/4 cup (50 mL) white wine vinegar and 2 tbsp (25 mL) lemon juice for red wine vinegar. Substitute 1 tbsp (15 mL) chopped fresh dill or 1 tsp (5 mL) dried dillweed for dried thyme.

Beef, Pork, Lamb and Veal

Lean, quick-cooking cuts of meat are great for fast and easy entrées. For simple burgers or a quick skillet supper, ground beef is versatile, economical and always a hit with younger family members. Our new variations on everyday beef and pork dishes, such as Chili with Chick-Peas, Baby Beef Liver with Yogurt-Mustard Sauce and Creole Ham and Rice, will get rave reviews from children and grown-ups alike. And in this section you'll also find simple yet elegant treatments for lamb and veal. In less than thirty minutes, you can serve Lamb Chops with Honey-Soy Glaze or Veal Chops with Green Peppercorns to guests, who'll think you've spent hours in the kitchen.

MINI MEAT LOAVES

If you are feeding only one or two, freeze the remaining loaves and sauce for future meals.

1	can (14 oz/398 mL) tomatoes	1
1-1/2 lb	lean ground beef	750 g
3/4 cup	chopped onions	175 mL
1 tbsp	Worcestershire sauce	15 mL
1 tsp	salt	5 mL
1/2 tsp	pepper	2 mL
1/2 tsp	dried basil	2 mL
BARBECUE SAUCE:		
	Liquid reserved from tomatoes	
2 tbsp	vinegar	25 mL
1 tbsp	chopped onion	15 mL
1 tbsp	packed brown sugar	15 mL
1 tsp	dry mustard	5 mL
1 tsp	Worcestershire sauce	5 mL
Dash	hot pepper sauce	Dash

• Drain tomatoes, reserving liquid for Barbecue Sauce. Mix together beef, tomatoes, onion, Worcestershire sauce, salt, pepper and basil; shape into 6 mini-loaves. Place on rack in baking pan; bake in 425°F (220°C) oven for 20 minutes or until meat is no longer pink.

• Meanwhile, in small saucepan, combine liquid reserved from tomatoes, vinegar, onion, sugar, mustard, Worcestershire sauce and hot pepper sauce; bring to boil. Reduce heat and simmer for 15 minutes. Serve spooned over meat loaves. Makes 6 servings.

• **Microwave Directions:** Prepare loaves as directed. Place shaped loaves in circle in 12-inch (30 cm) pie plate. Cover and microwave at High for 5 minutes. Drain off excess fat. Microwave, covered, at Medium (50%) for 6 minutes, rotating dish and rearranging loaves twice. Let stand, covered, while preparing sauce.

• **Barbecue Sauce:** Mix ingredients as directed above in a 4-cup (1 L) measure. Cover and microwave at High for 6 to 8 minutes or until mixture boils and thickens slightly, stirring once.

Mini Meat Loaf

SIRLOIN STEAK WITH WINE AND SHALLOT SAUCE

For fast company fare, start with Curried Squash Soup (recipe, p.54), then follow with this delicious sirloin steak and a salad of greens garnished with rose petals.

2	sirloin steaks (8 oz/250 g each), about 3/4 inch (2 cm) thick	2
2 tbsp	vegetable oil	25 mL
2	shallots, finely chopped	2
1/2 cup	red wine	125 mL
1/4 cup	beef stock	50 mL
2 tbsp	whipping cream	25 mL
	Salt and pepper	

• Trim excess fat from steaks; nick fat at 1-inch (2.5 cm) intervals. In heavy skillet, heat 1 tbsp (15 mL) of the oil over medium-high heat; cook steaks for 3 to 4 minutes on each side for medium-rare or until desired doneness. Transfer to plate and keep warm.
• Pour off excess fat from skillet. Reduce heat to medium and heat remaining oil; cook shallots, stirring, for about 1 minute or until softened.
• Add wine and stock, scraping up any brown bits. Bring to boil over high heat; cook for 2 to 3 minutes or until reduced to about 1/3 cup (75 mL).
• Strain sauce and return to skillet. Add cream and cook for 1 to 2 minutes or until thick enough to coat spoon. Stir in any accumulated meat juices from steaks. Season with salt and pepper to taste. Thinly slice steak and serve with sauce. Makes 4 servings.

Sirloin Steak with Wine and Shallot Sauce; Curried Squash Soup (p. 54)

STIR-FRIED BEEF WITH BROCCOLI

Steamed rice and gingered carrots are good accompaniments for this easy main dish. Finish with plum sorbet and almond cookies. A less expensive version can be made with flank steak if you can marinate the meat overnight or during the day. Just cover and refrigerate the beef mixture, stirring occasionally, for at least 2 hours or up to 8.

1 lb	sirloin steak	500 g
2	cloves garlic, minced	2
2 tbsp	soy sauce	25 mL
1	bunch broccoli	1
1/4 cup	vegetable or peanut oil	50 mL

• Cut beef with the grain into long strips 2 inches (5 cm) wide; cut crosswise into 1/2-inch (1 cm) wide strips. In small bowl, stir together beef, garlic and soy sauce. Cover and let marinate while preparing the broccoli.

• Cut broccoli into small florets. Peel and cut stems into 1-inch (2.5 cm) thick slices; set aside.

• Set wok over high heat for 30 seconds; add half of the oil and heat for 20 seconds. Stir in beef mixture; stir-fry for 3 to 4 minutes or until beef is no longer pink inside. Remove to bowl and keep warm.

• Heat remaining oil; add broccoli and stir-fry for 2 minutes. Add 2 tbsp (25 mL) water; reduce heat to low, cover and cook for 5 minutes. Return beef to pan and increase heat to high; stir-fry for 1 to 2 minutes or until beef is heated through and broccoli is tender but still crisp and bright green. Makes 4 servings.

BEEF PAILLARDS WITH DOUBLE PEPPER SAUCE

When the word "paillard" refers to beef, it usually means a thin steak, which can be taken from the sirloin, strip loin, rib or even the more economical top round. Quickly cooked either by pan-frying in a little fat or by grilling under the broiler or on the barbecue, the steaks are usually served rare. Accompany the steaks with a rice pilaf.

6	thin boneless steaks (3 to 6 oz/ 75 to 175 g each)	6
	Pepper	
1 tbsp	vegetable oil	15 mL
2 tbsp	chopped fresh basil or parsley	25 mL
	Vegetable oil for cooking	
DOUBLE PEPPER SAUCE:		
1 tbsp	vegetable oil	15 mL
1	small red onion, diced	1
1	clove garlic, finely chopped	1
1 tbsp	green peppercorns, crushed	15 mL
2	sweet red peppers, diced	2
1/2 cup	dry white wine or chicken stock	125 mL
	Salt	

• Season steaks lightly with pepper; brush with 1 tbsp (15 mL) oil. Set aside while preparing sauce.

• **Double Pepper Sauce:** In skillet, heat 1 tbsp (15 mL) oil over medium heat; cook onion, garlic and crushed peppercorns, stirring occasionally, for about 5 minutes or until onions are tender.

• Add red peppers to skillet and cook for about 5 minutes or until tender. Add wine and cook until liquid is reduced to about half. Season with salt to taste.

• **To pan-fry:** Brush large skillet with oil and heat over medium-high heat. Cook steaks, in batches, for 1 to 2 minutes per side or until desired doneness.

• **To broil:** Brush hot broiler pan with oil and heat for 2 minutes. Place steaks in pan and broil for 1 to 2 minutes per side or until desired doneness.

• **To barbecue:** Brush hot grill with oil and heat for 1 minute. Place steaks on grill and cook for 1 to 2 minutes per side or until desired doneness.

• Arrange steaks on individual plates. Spoon some of the sauce over each steak and sprinkle with basil. Makes 6 servings.

The names scallopini and paillards refer to thinly cut boneless slices of meat that have no fat or gristle. The thinness makes the meat extremely tender and preparation very fast. Paillards are usually under 1/4 inch (5 mm) thick. Scallopini are often pounded further to 1/8 inch (3 mm) or less.

BEEF-CABBAGE SKILLET DINNER

Serve this quick skillet supper with creamed potatoes and squash rings.

1 tbsp	vegetable oil	15 mL
1 lb	ground beef	500 g
1	onion, chopped	1
1	clove garlic, minced	1
1 tbsp	minced gingerroot	15 mL
6 cups	finely shredded cabbage (about 1 lb/500 g)	1.5 L
1/4 cup	chopped fresh parsley	50 mL
2 tbsp	soy sauce	25 mL

• In large skillet, heat oil over medium heat; cook beef, onion, garlic and gingerroot, breaking up meat with wooden spoon, for about 5 minutes or until browned.
• Stir in cabbage, parsley and soy sauce; cover and cook for 6 to 8 minutes or until cabbage is tender. Makes 4 servings.

CHILI WITH CHICK-PEAS

This easy-to-make, high-fibre dish is perfect when you have a group of teenagers with hearty appetites to feed.

1 lb	ground beef	500 g
2	onions, chopped	2
1	clove garlic, minced	1
2 tbsp	(approx) chili powder (or 1 dried chili pepper, crumbled)	25 mL
1	can (28 oz/796 mL) tomatoes	1
1	can (28 oz/796 mL) kidney beans, drained	1
1	can (19 oz/540 mL) chick-peas, drained	1
1	sweet red, yellow or green pepper, chopped	1
	Salt and pepper	

• In large heavy saucepan or skillet, cook beef over medium heat, stirring to break up meat, for about 5 minutes or until browned. Pour off any fat. Add onions, garlic and chili powder; cook until onions are tender.
• Stir in tomatoes, kidney beans, chick-peas and sweet pepper; bring to boil, reduce heat and simmer for 5 to 10 minutes or until flavors have blended. Season with salt, pepper and more chili powder to taste. Makes 6 to 8 servings.

CHILI BEEF BURGERS

Chili powder and cumin subtly accent these beef burgers. Try serving them topped with sour cream and wrapped in flour tortillas.

1	egg	1
1/4 cup	bread crumbs	50 mL
1/4 cup	finely chopped green onions	50 mL
2 tbsp	water	25 mL
1/2 tsp	each chili powder and salt	2 mL
1/4 tsp	each pepper, paprika and cumin	1 mL
Dash	hot pepper sauce	Dash
1 lb	ground beef	500 g

• In bowl, beat egg; stir in bread crumbs, onions, water, chili powder, salt, pepper, paprika, cumin and hot pepper sauce. Mix in beef; shape into 4 patties.
• Grill patties on greased grill 4 inches (10 cm) above medium-hot coals or on medium-high setting for about 10 minutes, turning once, or until desired doneness. (Alternatively, place on broiler pan about 4 inches/10 cm from heat and broil for 10 minutes, turning once, or until desired doneness.) Makes 4 servings.

BURGERS WITH SOUR CREAM SAUCE

Instead of the Blue Cheese Topping, spoon this delicious sour cream sauce over cooked patties and serve.

After cooking patties, pour off fat from skillet; add 1 tbsp (15 mL) each finely chopped shallots and red wine vinegar. Reduce heat to medium and cook, stirring, until vinegar has almost evaporated. Remove from heat; stir in 1/4 cup (50 mL) sour cream. Stir in 1 tbsp (15 mL) minced fresh parsley. Makes enough for 4 servings.

Burger with Sour Cream Sauce

BLUE CHEESE BURGERS

The addition of cream makes these beef patties wonderfully moist. When they're topped with a blue cheese and mustard combination, they are a cut above regular cheeseburgers. Serve the patties on toasted slices of French bread.

1 lb	regular ground beef	500 g
1/3 cup	whipping cream	75 mL
1/4 cup	dry bread crumbs	50 mL
1	small onion, finely chopped	1
1 tbsp	Worcestershire sauce	15 mL
1	clove garlic, minced	1
1 tsp	salt	5 mL
1/2 tsp	pepper	2 mL
2 tbsp	vegetable oil	25 mL
BLUE CHEESE TOPPING:		
1/4 cup	crumbled blue cheese	50 mL
2 tbsp	butter	25 mL
2 tsp	dry mustard	10 mL
Dash	Worcestershire sauce	Dash
Salt and peppper		

• In large bowl, combine beef, cream, bread crumbs, onion, Worcestershire sauce, garlic, salt and pepper. With moistened hands, mix well and form into 4, 6 or 8 patties, depending on desired thickness. (Cover and refrigerate for up to 8 hours, if making ahead.)

• In large heavy skillet, heat oil over medium-high heat; cook patties for 4 minutes on one side. Turn and cook for 2 minutes longer or until desired doneness and browned.

• **Blue Cheese Topping:** Meanwhile, in small bowl, cream together cheese, butter, mustard, Worcestershire sauce, and salt and pepper to taste.

• Spread over cooked patties; reduce heat to low and cook, covered, for about 2 minutes or until cheese has melted. Makes 4 servings.

NEW YORK PEPPER STEAK

Tender, lean steak is one of the fastest meats to cook when you're in a hurry. Pepper adds a piquant zip and mushrooms dress up the dish. If whole peppercorns are not available, use a very coarse grinding of black pepper.

4	New York strip steaks (about 6 oz/170 g each)	4
1/4 cup	olive oil	50 mL
1 tbsp	whole peppercorns, crushed	15 mL
1/2 lb	mushrooms, halved	250 g

• Trim steaks and brush each with 1 tbsp (15 mL) oil. Press peppercorns into both sides of steaks; place on broiler pan.
• Broil steaks for 5 minutes; turn steaks over. Arrange mushrooms around steaks; broil for 5 minutes longer for medium doneness. Makes 4 servings.

BEEF NOODLE STOVE-TOP CASSEROLE

This flavorful one-pot supper is very easy for rush hour because the noodles don't have to be cooked separately. It's also great for cottage or galley cooking, and a sure crowd-pleaser après ski.

1-1/2 lb	ground beef	750 g
1-1/2 cups	chopped onion	375 mL
1 cup	chopped celery	250 mL
1/2 cup	chopped sweet green pepper	125 mL
1 tsp	salt	5 mL
1/4 tsp	pepper	1 mL
1	can (19 oz/540 mL) tomatoes	1
1	can (19 oz/540 mL) tomato juice	1
1	can (19 oz/ 540 mL) red kidney beans (undrained)	1
1	can (10 oz/ 284 mL) mushroom pieces (undrained)	1
1 tbsp	chili powder	15 mL
1/3 lb	uncooked broad noodles	175 g

• In a very large heavy pot or Dutch oven, brown ground beef. Add onion, celery, green pepper, salt and pepper. Cook, stirring often, until vegetables are softened. Drain off any excess fat.
• Add tomatoes, tomato juice, kidney beans, mushrooms and chili powder. Bring to boil; stir in noodles. Reduce heat, cover and simmer for about 15 minutes or until noodles are tender. Taste and adjust seasoning if necessary. Makes about 8 servings.

Baby Beef Liver with Yogurt-Mustard Sauce

BABY BEEF LIVER WITH YOGURT-MUSTARD SAUCE

Keep liver in mind when you're dashing into the supermarket just before dinner. It's one of the original fast foods and is best cooked quickly and on the day it is bought.

1/2 cup	plain yogurt or sour cream	125 mL
2 tsp	Dijon mustard	10 mL
1/2 tsp	Worcestershire sauce	2 mL
1 lb	baby beef liver	500 g
2 tbsp	all-purpose flour	25 mL
2 tbsp	butter	25 mL
2	onions, chopped	2
2 tbsp	water	25 mL
	Salt and pepper	

• Combine yogurt, mustard and Worcestershire sauce; mix well and set aside. Dredge liver in flour.

• In large heavy skillet, melt butter over medium heat; cook onions for 2 minutes. Increase heat to high and sauté liver for 1 to 2 minutes on each side or until liver is light pink inside.

• Remove liver to hot platter. Pour water into pan and stir to scrape up any brown bits. Remove from heat and stir in yogurt mixture; season with salt and pepper to taste. Spoon sauce over liver. Makes 4 servings.

BEEF TERIYAKI WITH SWEET-AND-SOUR VEGETABLES

It takes very little time to prepare this tasty Japanese-style meal.

Japanese wheat flour noodles and dipping sauces are perfect accompaniments for Beef Teriyaki with Sweet-and-Sour Vegetables (see our photograph). Just drop noodles into pot of boiling salted water a minute before cooking the meat. They'll be ready to drain and serve when the beef is cooked. For dipping sauces, spoon plum sauce, hot mustard and teriyaki sauce (with a dash of rice wine or dry sherry) into small bowls.

3/4 lb	boneless strip loin steak	375 g
1 tbsp	plum sauce	15 mL
1 tsp	teriyaki sauce	5 mL
1	large clove garlic, crushed	1
5	thin slices gingerroot	5
1 tbsp	peanut oil	15 mL
VEGETABLES:		
Half	small head red cabbage	Half
1	large carrot	1
1	small cucumber	1
2 tbsp	vegetable oil	25 mL
2 tbsp	rice or sherry vinegar	25 mL
1 tsp	packed brown sugar	5 mL
1 tsp	teriyaki sauce	5 mL
1/4 tsp	ginger	1 mL
Pinch	ground coriander	Pinch

- **Vegetables:** In food processor or by hand, coarsely grate cabbage, carrot and cucumber. (Pat cucumber with paper towels to absorb excess moisture.) Mound vegetables separately in shallow serving dish.
- Whisk together oil, vinegar, sugar, teriyaki sauce, ginger and coriander. Drizzle over vegetables and set aside.
- Slice steak thinly across the grain. Toss with plum and teriyaki sauces; set aside.
- In heavy skillet, cook garlic, gingerroot and peanut oil over medium-low heat for 3 minutes. Remove and discard garlic and gingerroot.
- Increase heat to high and add beef mixture to skillet; cook, tossing lightly, for about 1-1/2 minutes or until beef is browned. Arrange on serving plate and pass vegetables separately. Makes 4 servings.

CHEESE-TOPPED PORK CHOPS

Serve with broiled potato slices, steamed broccoli and, for dessert, poached pears with whipped cream.

4	thick loin pork chops	4
	Pepper	
1 cup	shredded Gruyère cheese (about 1/4 lb/ 125 g)	250 mL
2 tbsp	Dijon mustard	25 mL
2	tomatoes, halved	2

- Trim fat from chops and cook fat in large ovenproof skillet over high heat until rendered (liquid). Remove and discard crisp bits.
- In rendered fat in pan, brown chops quickly. Season with pepper to taste. Reduce heat to medium-low and cook for about 20 minutes or until cooked through, turning once. Drain off any excess fat.
- Combine cheese and mustard to form paste; spread evenly over each chop. Place tomato halves around chops and broil until cheese melts and tomatoes are heated through, about 5 minutes. Makes 4 servings.

Beef Teriyaki with Sweet-and-Sour Vegetables; Japanese noodles; dipping sauces

ONE POTATO—TWO POTATO AND CHOPS

This is a perfect meal for meat and potato fans. While it simmers, toss grated carrots with poppy seeds and sprinkle with oil, lemon juice, brown sugar, salt and pepper.

4	pork rib or loin chops (1 to 1-1/2 lb/500 to 750 g total)	4
2	onions, cut in 1/4-inch (5 mm) thick slices	2
4	potatoes, cut in 1/4-inch (5 mm) thick slices	4
2	firm red apples, cored and cut in 1/4-inch (5 mm) thick slices	2
1	large sweet potato, peeled and cut in 1/4-inch (5 mm) thick slices	1
1 cup	chicken stock	250 mL
	Salt and pepper	

• Trim some of the fat from chops and place in cold skillet; cook over medium heat for about 3 minutes to render drippings. Discard trimmings.
• Add chops to skillet and brown in drippings for 3 to 4 minutes on each side; push to side of pan.
• Add onions to skillet; cook for about 5 minutes or until tender and translucent. Add potatoes, apples and sweet potato; toss gently and arrange pork chops on top. Pour stock over and bring to boil; reduce heat, cover and simmer for 30 minutes.
• Uncover and simmer for 5 to 10 minutes longer or until stock is reduced and vegetables are tender. Season with salt and pepper to taste. Makes 4 servings.

PORK CHOPS IN BEER WITH SAUERKRAUT

Beer and tomato juice add hearty flavor to pork, and sauerkraut is a traditional accompaniment. In this recipe, they are all cooked in the same skillet. The sauce is also ideal for less tender shoulder chops; just increase the cooking time and add a little more liquid, if needed. Serve with dark rye bread, German mustard and pickled beets or dills.

2 tbsp	vegetable oil	25 mL
4	pork chops	4
	Salt and pepper	
1 tbsp	packed brown sugar	15 mL
1	onion, sliced	1
1/2 cup	beer	125 mL
1/2 cup	tomato juice	125 mL
1	can (28 oz/796 mL) sauerkraut, drained	1
1 tsp	caraway seeds (optional)	5 mL

• In skillet, heat oil and brown chops on both sides. Sprinkle lightly with salt and pepper; sprinkle with brown sugar.
• Add onion, beer and tomato juice; cover and simmer for 5 minutes. Uncover and simmer for about 15 minutes or until liquid is reduced and thickened slightly.
• Remove chops and sauce; set aside. Spread sauerkraut in skillet; sprinkle with caraway seeds (if using). Arrange chops on top of sauerkraut; spoon sauce over. Cover and simmer for about 10 minutes or until chops are tender. Makes 4 servings.

One Potato—Two Potato and Chops

HURRY CURRY

In this quick version of curry, stir-fried pork and vegetables are simmered in a tomato-based sauce.

1 lb	pork tenderloin	500 g
2	onions	2
1	stalk celery	1
1 tbsp	butter	15 mL
1 tbsp	vegetable oil	15 mL
1	can (7-1/2 oz/ 213 mL) tomato sauce	1
1 tbsp	curry powder	15 mL
1/2 tsp	packed brown sugar	2 mL
1/2 tsp	salt	2 mL
2 tbsp	flaked coconut	25 mL

• Slice pork into 1-1/2-inch (4 cm) long strips about 1/2 inch (1 cm) wide. Coarsely chop onions and celery.
• In large skillet, melt butter with oil over medium-high heat; stir-fry pork for 3 to 4 minutes or until browned. Add onions and celery; stir-fry for 2 minutes.
• Stir in tomato sauce, curry powder, sugar and salt; bring to boil, reduce heat and simmer for 4 minutes. Sprinkle coconut over individual servings. Makes 4 servings.

CREOLE HAM AND RICE

This tomato, ham and rice combo is a good example of carefree cooking at its best. While it's simmering, warm cornmeal muffins.

4	strips bacon	4
2	onions, chopped	2
1	can (28 oz/ 796 mL) tomatoes (undrained)	1
1 cup	cubed cooked ham	250 mL
1 cup	long-grain rice	250 mL
1	small sweet green pepper, seeded and chopped	1
	Salt and pepper	

• In skillet, cook bacon over medium heat, turning once, for 3 to 4 minutes or until crisp. Remove and drain on paper towels.
• To skillet, add onions and cook for about 5 minutes or until tender and translucent.
• Stir in tomatoes, ham, rice and green pepper; bring to boil, reduce heat, cover and simmer for 15 minutes or until rice is tender. Season with salt and pepper to taste.
• Crumble bacon and sprinkle over creole. Makes 4 servings.

Whether you're serving Hurry Curry or Creole Ham and Rice, take advantage of the simmering time to toss thin celery and carrot slices with alfalfa sprouts and raisins for a refreshing salad. For dessert, serve icy cold papaya or mango slices.

BROILING

Broiling is a fast and simple way of using high heat to cook tender lean cuts of meat. Remember that some fat marbling adds to the meat's flavor and tenderness. Fat will melt and drip off as the meat cooks. Slash any exterior fat before broiling to prevent curling.

Test for doneness by touch as well as timing. Use the flat of a fork or your finger to avoid piercing the meat and letting juices escape. For well done, meat is firm; for medium, it springs back; for rare, meat is soft to the touch. Broil meat on a rack or in a pan 4 to 6 inches (10 to 15 cm) below the heat; season with salt afterward to minimize drying out.

Thin cuts of meat have to be watched carefully when broiling to avoid overcooking and drying out. Do not buy wedge-cut steaks and chops that are thick on one side and thin on the other. These will cook unevenly under the broiler. Most meats that are broiled can also be grilled on a barbecue over direct heat. Cooking times will vary due to outdoor temperatures, winds and how hot your fire is (if using charcoal).

PORK TENDERLOIN WITH MUSTARD-PEPPERCORN CRUST

This dish is elegant enough for company when served with rice pilaf and steamed carrots and snow peas. The recipe can be easily doubled.

3/4 lb	pork tenderloin, trimmed	375 g
1 tbsp	**Dijon mustard**	15 mL
1/2 tsp	**dried thyme**	2 mL
2 tsp	**crushed black peppercorns**	10 mL

• Pat tenderloin dry. Mix together mustard and thyme; spread all over tenderloin. Sprinkle all over with peppercorns.

• Place on rack in roasting pan and roast in 400°F (200°C) oven for 30 to 40 minutes or until meat thermometer inserted into thickest part registers 160-170°F (71-75°C) and juices run clear. To serve, cut into 3/4-inch (2 cm) thick slices. Makes 2 to 4 servings.

• **Microwave Directions:** Microwave browning grill at High for 5 minutes or according to manufacturer's instructions. Add 1 tsp (5 mL) vegetable oil and tilt to coat evenly. Add prepared tenderloin and microwave at High for 5 to 8 minutes or until no longer pink inside, rotating dish 3 times during cooking. Transfer to serving plate and tent loosely with foil. Let stand for 5 minutes before slicing.

PORK CHOPS WITH PINK PEARS

Cranberries and poached pears with pork chops is a delightful combination of flavors. Poach the pears as the pork chops cook. Be sure to trim all visible fat from the chops.

4	loin pork chops	4
1/3 cup	chicken stock	75 mL
1/4 cup	maple syrup	50 mL
	Salt and pepper	
1 tsp	cornstarch	5 mL
	Pears in Wine (recipe opposite page)	
1/2 cup	cranberries, fresh or frozen (optional)	125 mL

Pork Chops with Pink Pears

• In lightly greased skillet, cook pork over medium-high heat for 2 to 3 minutes per side or until lightly browned. Add stock and maple syrup; cook, partially covered, over low heat for 12 to 15 minutes or until chops are cooked through (no longer pink in centre when cut). Season with salt and pepper to taste.

• Remove chops to serving platter; keep warm. Return skillet to medium-high heat; bring pan juices to boil. Dissolve cornstarch in 2 tbsp (25 mL) cold water. Add to skillet and cook, stirring, for 2 minutes or until thickened.

• Using slotted spoon, transfer pears from Pears in Wine to skillet; add cranberries (if using) and cook for 3 minutes or until cranberries are tender and pears are heated through. Arrange around chops; spoon sauce over. Makes 4 servings.

PEARS IN WINE:

2	firm pears, peeled	2
3/4 cup	red wine	175 mL
1/4 cup	granulated sugar	50 mL
1	stick cinnamon	1
3	whole cloves	3
1	strip lemon rind	1
	Red food coloring (optional)	

• Halve pears and remove cores. Place in saucepan; add wine, sugar, cinnamon, cloves and lemon rind. Bring to boil; reduce heat and simmer, covered, for 10 to 15 minutes or just until pears are tender. Add a few drops food coloring (if using). Cover and set aside while preparing chops.

• **Microwave Directions:** In shallow dish, mix together wine, sugar, cinnamon, cloves and lemon rind. Microwave, covered, at High for 1 to 2 minutes or until boiling. Add halved and cored pears. Microwave at High for 4 to 5 minutes or until pears are tender, turning and rearranging pears once. Cover and let stand while preparing chops.

Be flexible. With slight adjustments in cooking times, you can substitute:
• lamb or veal chops for pork chops in Pork Chops with Pink Pears.
• lean, tender chunks of beef, lamb or chicken breasts for pork tenderloin in Pork and Red Pepper Shish Kabobs.
• veal or turkey cutlets for pork cutlets in Pork Cutlets with Kiwi.

PORK AND RED PEPPER SHISH KABOBS

For a quick easy meal, accompany with buttered noodles or rice and serve ice cream for dessert. Lamb or chicken can be substituted for the pork. If time permits, marinate the pork overnight for even more flavor.

1 lb	pork tenderloin	500 g
2	sweet red peppers	2
1/3 cup	olive oil	75 mL
3 tbsp	lemon juice	50 mL
1 tbsp	chopped fresh rosemary (or 1/2 tsp/2 mL dried)	15 mL
1 tbsp	Dijon mustard	15 mL
1/2 tsp	salt	2 mL
1/4 tsp	pepper	1 mL

• Trim fat from pork; cut meat into 1-1/2-inch (4 cm) cubes. Halve red peppers; remove and discard seeds and ribs. Cut peppers into 1-1/2-inch (4 cm) squares.

• In bowl, mix together olive oil, lemon juice, rosemary, mustard, salt and pepper. Add pork and red peppers, stirring to coat well; marinate for at least 15 minutes or refrigerate overnight. Drain and reserve marinade in saucepan.

• Alternately thread meat and red peppers onto 4 long or 8 short skewers. (If using wooden skewers, soak in cold water for 10 minutes before using to prevent scorching.) Broil or grill kabobs, turning every 2 to 3 minutes, for 10 to 12 minutes or until pork is no longer pink inside.

• Meanwhile, bring marinade to boil; brush on shish kabobs halfway through cooking time. Makes about 4 servings.

PORK CUTLETS WITH KIWI

This is a fast and easy dish with only 5 ingredients. Make sure the kiwifruit is ripe (not sour) but firm.

4	pork cutlets (about 1 lb/ 500 g), trimmed	4
2 tbsp	butter	25 mL
1/4 tsp	coarse black pepper	1 mL
2	kiwifruit, peeled and sliced	2
2 tbsp	toasted sliced almonds	25 mL

• Pound cutlets very thin. In large skillet, heat butter over medium-high heat; sauté cutlets quickly just until golden, turning once. Sprinkle with pepper and transfer to heated platter; keep warm.

• Reduce heat to medium-low and add kiwi slices and almonds to skillet; toss gently in pan juices just until heated through. Gently spoon onto cutlets. Makes 4 servings.

PORK MEDALLIONS WITH CRANBERRY-PORT SAUCE

*Pork Medallions with
Cranberry-Port Sauce*

*The easy cranberry sauce is a fine
complement to the pork.*

1 lb	pork tenderloin	500 g
1	egg	1
2 tbsp	water	25 mL
3/4 cup	fine cracker crumbs	175 mL
1 tbsp	butter	15 mL
1 tbsp	vegetable oil	15 mL
CRANBERRY-PORT SAUCE:		
1/2 cup	cranberry sauce	125 mL
2 tbsp	port	25 mL

• Slice pork into 3/4-inch (2 cm) thick slices; place between 2 sheets of waxed paper and pound to 1/4-inch (5 mm) thickness.

• In shallow dish, beat egg with water. Place cracker crumbs in separate dish. Dip pork into egg mixture; press into crumbs and set aside.

• In skillet, melt butter with oil over medium-high heat; cook pork for about 3 minutes on each side or until golden brown.

• **Cranberry-Port Sauce:** In microwaveable bowl, mix together cranberry sauce and port. Cover with vented plastic wrap and microwave at High for about 1 minute or until heated through. (Alternatively, heat in saucepan over medium heat until heated through.) Pass sauce separately. Makes 4 servings.

BANGERS WITH ONIONS AND APPLES

Onion and apple slices cook along with the sausage for a tasty combination. Serve with dark pumpernickel bread or microwaved small potatoes topped with sour cream.

2 tbsp	vegetable oil	25 mL
1 lb	breakfast sausages	500 g
4	red onions	4
2	large apples	2
2 tbsp	packed brown sugar	25 mL
1/2 tsp	cinnamon	2 mL
1/2 cup	water	125 mL

• In large skillet, heat oil over medium-high heat; cook sausages, turning frequently, for 4 minutes.
• Quarter and slice onions. Peel and slice apples. Add onions and apples to skillet; cook, stirring occasionally, for about 5 minutes or until onions are tender. Sprinkle with sugar and cinnamon; pour in water.
• Reduce heat to low, cover and simmer for about 5 minutes or until sausages are cooked through. Makes 4 servings.

PORK TENDERLOIN WITH MUSTARD AND HERBS

Pork tenderloin is an ideal choice when you want to spend a minimum amount of time in preparation, yet can afford to wait the 40 minutes it takes to cook.

1 lb	pork tenderloin	500 g
2 tbsp	Dijon mustard	25 mL
1/2 cup	fine fresh bread crumbs	125 mL
1 tsp	each dried thyme, basil and oregano	5 mL
1 tsp	salt	5 mL
1/4 tsp	pepper	1 mL

• Spread pork tenderloin with mustard. In shallow dish, combine bread crumbs, thyme, basil, oregano, salt and pepper; mix well. Roll tenderloin in crumb mixture.
• Roast on baking sheet in 350°F (180°C) oven for 40 minutes or until meat thermometer registers 160–170°F (71–75°C) and juices run clear. Remove from oven and let stand for 5 minutes. Cut into thin slices to serve. Makes 4 servings.

Pork Tenderloin with Mustard and Herbs

Long-grain white rice is perfect simply buttered and served as a side dish with any meat entrée. To cook: Add rice to twice its volume of boiling water (salted if desired); cover, reduce heat to low and cook for 15 minutes or until grains are tender and water has been absorbed. Let stand for 5 minutes, then fluff with a fork.

BRATWURST SKILLET SUPPER

Team this fast dish with dark bread, a grainy mustard and pickled beets for a hearty supper on a cold wintry day.

1 lb	**bratwurst sausages**	500 g
3 cups	**shredded cabbage**	750 mL
1	**large apple (unpeeled), cored and diced**	1
1/4 cup	**apple juice or chicken stock**	50 mL
1 tsp	**caraway seeds**	5 mL
	Salt and pepper	

• In large skillet, cook sausage over medium heat for 12 to 15 minutes or until browned. Drain off excess fat.

• Add cabbage, apple, apple juice, caraway seeds, and salt and pepper to taste; toss lightly. Cover and reduce heat to low; cook for about 10 minutes or until sausages are cooked through and cabbage is tender-crisp.

• Uncover and cook, stirring, for 3 to 4 minutes or until most of the liquid has evaporated. Makes 4 servings.

Bratwurst Skillet Supper

SAUSAGE PATTIES WITH MUSTARD CREAM

Serve these tasty patties with a bright green vegetable such as peas, green beans or lima beans. For dessert, sprinkle coconut on fresh orange slices.

1 lb	sausage meat	500 g
1	egg	1
1/2 tsp	each dried thyme and sage	2 mL
	Pepper	
1/4 cup	all-purpose flour	50 mL
MUSTARD CREAM:		
1/3 cup	whipping cream, whipped	75 mL
3 tbsp	mayonnaise	50 mL
2 tbsp	Dijon mustard	25 mL
1 tbsp	horseradish	15 mL

• In bowl, mix together sausage meat, egg, thyme, sage, and pepper to taste. Place flour in shallow dish. Drop sausage mixture, 1/4 cup (50 mL) at a time, into flour; flatten slightly to make patties, coating both sides with flour.

• In lightly greased skillet, cook patties over medium heat for 3 to 4 minutes per side or until browned on outside and centres are no longer pink.

• **Mustard Cream:** In bowl, blend together whipped cream, mayonnaise, mustard and horseradish. Serve with sausage patties. Makes 4 servings.

For a change of pace, use fresh Farmer's, Italian or Weisswurst (pork and veal) sausages instead of bratwurst. Save even more time by using precooked sausage in Bratwurst Skillet Supper. Choose from:
• *Bockwurst—with spicy ground veal*
• *Debreczner—Hungarian, spicy, paprika-colored ground pork filling*
• *Frankfurter—beef, pork, veal or chicken*
• *Kielbasa—Polish, lightly smoked ham or chicken*
• *Pepperoni—spicy beef and pork*
• *Thuringer—like frankfurters but a coarser grind of pork or veal*

CURRIED LAMB CHOPS

Make this fast and easy curry sauce as spicy as you like. Serve with rice and a cool cucumber salad.

2 tbsp	butter	25 mL
8 to 12	lamb loin chops	8 to 12
1	small onion	1
1	small apple, peeled and cored	1
1	small stalk celery	1
2	cloves garlic	2
2 tbsp	(approx) curry powder	25 mL
1/4 tsp	dried thyme	1 mL
1 cup	chicken stock	250 mL
1/2 cup	chopped canned tomatoes	125 mL
	Salt and pepper	

• In skillet, melt butter and brown chops on both sides; remove and set aside.

• Meanwhile, in food processor or by hand, finely chop onion, apple, celery and garlic; cook in same skillet until softened but not browned.

• Stir in curry powder and thyme; cook, stirring, for 1 minute. Stir in chicken stock and tomatoes; simmer for 2 minutes. Season with salt and pepper to taste; add more curry powder if desired. For a smooth sauce, purée in food processor and pour back into skillet.

• Return chops to skillet; cover and simmer until chops are tender, about 10 minutes, adding a little more stock or water if too thick. Makes 4 servings.

LAMB CHOPS WITH HONEY-SOY GLAZE

The honey-soy glaze gives these lamb chops a subtle sweet flavor. You can use any of today's soy sauces—regular, light or salt-reduced—in this recipe. Teriyaki sauce can be used in place of soy sauce.

8	lamb loin chops (about 1-1/2 lb/ 750 g total)	8
1/4 cup	ketchup	50 mL
2 tbsp	liquid honey	25 mL
1 tbsp	soy sauce	15 mL
1 tsp	minced gingerroot	5 mL
1	clove garlic, minced	1

• Trim chops and pat dry.
• In large bowl, combine ketchup, honey, soy sauce, gingerroot and garlic; add lamb chops and turn to coat well.
• Remove chops from sauce reserving any remaining sauce and broil chops about 4 inches (10 cm) from heat for 4 minutes. Turn chops and brush with sauce. Broil for 4 minutes longer or until well browned, juicy and pink inside. Makes 4 servings.

LAMB CHOPS CREOLE

This delicious casserole tastes just as good when made with pork chops. To double the recipe, use a 6- to 8-cup (1.5 to 2 L) casserole or baking dish.

3/4 lb	shoulder, rib or loin lamb chops, about 3/4 inch (2 cm) thick	375 g
1 tsp	vegetable oil	5 mL
1/2 cup	chopped onion	125 mL
1/2 cup	chopped celery	125 mL
1/2 cup	chopped sweet green pepper	125 mL
1 cup	canned tomatoes, coarsely chopped	250 mL
1/2 cup	long-grain rice	125 mL
1/2 cup	chicken stock or water	125 mL
1/4 tsp	salt	1 mL
Dash	hot pepper sauce	Dash

• Trim any excess fat from chops. In deep heavy skillet, heat oil over medium-high heat; cook chops for about 4 minutes on each side or until browned. Remove from pan and set aside.
• In same skillet, cook onion, celery and green pepper over medium heat until softened, about 5 minutes. Stir in tomatoes, rice, stock, salt and hot pepper sauce; bring just to boil, stirring constantly.
• Remove from heat and transfer to greased 4-cup (1 L) casserole or baking dish. Top with lamb chops. Bake, covered, in 350°F (180°C) oven for 30 to 35 minutes or until rice has absorbed all liquid and chops are tender. Makes 2 servings.

CARAWAY VEGETABLE PLATTER

Microwave this tasty vegetable side dish to serve with Lamb Chops with Honey-Soy Glaze.

Arrange 1-1/2 cups (375 mL) thinly sliced carrots in ring around outside of 10-inch (25 cm) plate or shallow dish. Arrange 1-1/2 cups (375 mL) finely cubed white turnip in ring inside carrots. Mound 1 cup (250 mL) trimmed snow peas in centre. Sprinkle vegetables with 2 tbsp (25 mL) water. Cover with vented plastic wrap and microwave at High for 3 to 5 minutes or just until vegetables are tender-crisp, rotating plate once. In 1-cup (250 mL) measure, microwave 2 tbsp (25 mL) butter at High for 30 to 60 seconds or until melted. Stir in 1/2 tsp (2 mL) caraway seeds. Drain water from vegetables without disturbing arrangement; drizzle with butter mixture. Season with salt and pepper to taste. Makes 4 servings.

Lamb Chops with Honey-Soy Glaze

GRILLED LAMB CHOPS WITH HERB BUTTER

For a special treat, spread herbed butter over grilled or broiled lamb chops. You could also use coriander or cumin to flavor the butter.

10	loin lamb chops, cut 1 inch (2.5 cm) thick	10
2	cloves garlic, halved	2
HERB BUTTER:		
2 tbsp	butter, softened	25 mL
1 tbsp	chopped fresh rosemary or oregano (or 1/2 tsp/2 mL dried)	15 mL
1 tsp	lemon juice	5 mL

• **Herb Butter:** In small dish, combine butter, rosemary and lemon juice; mix well and set aside.
• Rub both sides of lamb chops with cut side of garlic. Place chops on greased rack 4 to 6 inches (10 to 15 cm) from medium-hot coals or on medium-high setting; grill for 3 to 5 minutes on each side for rare, 7 to 8 minutes for medium. (Alternatively, broil lamb chops 3 inches/8 cm from heat for 5 to 6 minutes per side for medium.)
• Spread one side of each chop with a little herb butter and serve immediately. Makes 5 servings.

LAMB PATTIES IN PITA ROUNDS

Ground lamb patties are a tasty alternative to hamburgers. Instead of frying the patties, you can barbecue or broil them if you like. Serve with traditional hamburger trimmings, or, for variety, add yogurt and chutney to buns or pita rounds. Complete the meal with a large platter of raw vegetables such as green beans, zucchini and sweet peppers. Serve with Hummus (recipe, p. 34).

1 lb	ground lamb	500 g
1/2 cup	chopped fresh parsley	125 mL
1	onion, minced	1
1/2 tsp	paprika	2 mL
1/4 tsp	cinnamon	1 mL
	Salt and pepper	
4	pita breads	4

• In bowl, mix together lamb, parsley, onion, paprika, cinnamon, and salt and pepper to taste; shape mixture into 4 patties.
• In lightly greased skillet, cook patties for 3 to 5 minutes on each side or until desired doneness and browned. To serve, place patties inside pita breads. Makes 4 servings.

FRESH MINTED SALSA

Serve this salsa with Lamb Patties in Pita Rounds instead of the Hummus, if you like. Combine 1 tsp (5 mL) vegetable oil, 2 chopped green onions and 1 minced garlic clove. Cook over medium-high heat for 2 to 3 minutes or until barely softened. (Alternatively, microwave at High for 1 minute.) Add half of a seedless cucumber, finely diced, 2 seeded and chopped tomatoes, 2 tbsp (25 mL) chopped fresh mint, a dash of hot pepper sauce, and salt and pepper to taste. Stir together; spoon over lamb patties in pitas. Makes 2 cups (500 mL).

Lamb Hot Pot

LAMB HOT POT

Once this savory stew is simmering in its pot, there's plenty of time to toss a simple salad to go with it. Just add a basket of crusty rolls for a complete meal.

1 lb	lamb shoulder, trimmed	500 g
1 tsp	olive oil	5 mL
1/2 cup	chopped onion	125 mL
1	clove garlic, minced	1
1 cup	chicken stock	250 mL
1-1/2 cups	cubed potatoes	375 mL
1/2 cup	each cubed carrot and turnip	125 mL
1 tsp	crushed dried rosemary	5 mL
1 cup	peas, fresh or frozen	250 mL
	Salt and pepper	
	Chopped fresh parsley	

• Cut lamb into 1-inch (2.5 cm) cubes. In heavy saucepan or Dutch oven, heat oil over medium-high heat; sauté lamb for about 4 minutes or until browned. Remove with slotted spoon and set aside.

• Add onion and garlic to pan; cook for about 3 minutes or until softened. Stir in stock and return lamb to pan; bring to boil. Reduce heat, cover and simmer for 10 minutes.

• Add potatoes, carrot, turnip and rosemary; simmer for about 20 minutes or until lamb and vegetables are tender. Add peas and simmer until heated through. Season with salt and pepper to taste; sprinkle with parsley. Makes 4 servings.

SCHNITZELLED CHOPS OR CHICKEN

This is a good way to prepare thin chops or boneless chicken breasts because the short cooking keeps them moist and tender. A classic schnitzel using very thin veal or pork cutlets cooks fastest, but you can use any tender chops, bone-in or boneless. For variety, season the crumbs with dried herbs.

4 to 8	thin chops (veal, pork or lamb) or chicken breasts	4 to 8
1	egg, lightly beaten	1
	Fine dry bread crumbs	
1/4 cup	vegetable oil (half butter if desired)	50 mL
	Salt and pepper	
	Lemon wedges	

• Dip chops into egg, then bread crumbs to coat lightly and evenly.
• In skillet, heat oil over medium-high heat; brown meat on both sides, sprinkling with salt and pepper to taste.
• Reduce heat and cook for 1 to 3 minutes on each side or just until cooked through. Do not overcook. Serve garnished with lemon wedges. Makes 4 servings.

Veal Chops with Green Peppercorns

VEAL SCALLOPINI IN MUSHROOM MADEIRA SAUCE

A simple but stylish sauce over quickly cooked meat makes classy rush-hour fare. Use pork or turkey scallopini for a change of flavor.

1 lb	veal scallops	500 g
	All-purpose flour	
1 tbsp	vegetable oil	15 mL
2 tbsp	(approx) butter	25 mL
1/2 lb	small mushrooms, cut in half	250 g
2 tbsp	minced shallots or onion	25 mL
2	cloves garlic, minced	2
1/2 cup	beef stock	125 mL
1/4 cup	Madeira	50 mL
1/2 cup	whipping cream	125 mL
	Salt and pepper	
2 tbsp	chopped fresh parsley	25 mL

• Using flat side of meat cleaver, pound veal very thin between 2 sheets of waxed paper. Dust veal lightly with flour.
• In large skillet, heat oil with 1 tbsp (15 mL) of the butter over medium-high heat; cook veal (in batches if necessary) for about 1 minute on each side or until lightly browned. Remove veal; set aside.
• Melt remaining butter in skillet; cook mushrooms, stirring, for about 3 minutes or just until tender, adding a little more butter if needed. Remove with slotted spoon and set aside with veal.
• To juices in pan, add shallots and garlic; cook briefly until softened, about 1 minute. Stir in stock and Madeira; cook until reduced by half, about 2 minutes. Add any juice that has accumulated around veal and mushrooms; pour in cream.
• Reduce again to thicken slightly, about 1 minute. Season with salt and pepper to taste. Add veal, mushrooms and parsley; heat through. Makes 4 servings.

VEAL CHOPS WITH GREEN PEPPERCORNS

Green peppercorns are soft edible berries that are especially popular with people who love pepper.

6	veal chops	6
3 tbsp	unsalted butter or vegetable oil	50 mL
1	small onion, chopped	1
1	clove garlic, finely chopped	1
3 tbsp	green peppercorns, crushed	50 mL
1/2 cup	dry red wine	125 mL
1/4 cup	chopped fresh parsley	50 mL

• Pat veal chops dry; trim any excess fat.
• In large skillet, heat butter over medium-high heat and cook veal for 5 to 7 minutes on each side or until well browned and cooked through. Remove veal to serving platter; discard any fat in skillet and return pan to heat.
• Add onion, garlic and peppercorns to skillet. Pour in wine and stir to scrape up any bits of veal from bottom of pan. Cook over medium-high heat until liquid is reduced to 3 tbsp (50 mL); add parsley. Pour sauce over veal. Makes 6 servings.

Poultry

Chicken is the answer to a busy cook's prayers. It's one of the fastest meats to cook, especially if you start with boneless chicken breasts. Speedy techniques—sautéing, stir-frying, broiling, microwaving and barbecuing—are ideal for chicken pieces. Choose recipes such as Lemon Chicken, Chicken and Apple Sauté or Chicken and Red Pepper Stir-Fry to get out of the kitchen fast. And don't ignore turkey for tasty, no-fuss dinners. Herb-Grilled Turkey Scallopini and Turkey Cutlets with Lemon and Rosemary make delicious meals even when it's not a holiday.

CHICKEN AND RED PEPPER STIR-FRY

Take advantage of the super-quick stir-fry method to cook this colorful chicken dish. Serve it on a bed of steamed rice. The recipe can be easily doubled to serve 4.

2	boneless skinless chicken breasts	2
1	sweet red pepper	1
1	orange	1
2 tbsp	chicken stock or water	25 mL
1 tbsp	soy sauce	15 mL
1 tsp	granulated sugar	5 mL
1 tsp	cornstarch	5 mL
1/2 tsp	sesame oil	2 mL
Dash	hot pepper sauce	Dash
2 tbsp	vegetable oil	25 mL
2 tsp	minced gingerroot	10 mL
1	clove garlic, minced	1

• Cut chicken into thin 2-inch (5 cm) long strips; set aside. Cut red pepper into similar strips; set aside. Using vegetable peeler, remove thin orange rind and cut into julienne strips; set aside.

• Squeeze orange and reserve 1/4 cup (50 mL) juice in small bowl. Stir in chicken stock, soy sauce, sugar, cornstarch, sesame oil and hot pepper sauce; set aside.

• In wok or large skillet, heat 1 tbsp (15 mL) of the oil over high heat. Stir-fry chicken for 3 to 4 minutes or until no longer pink inside. Remove chicken and set aside. Heat remaining oil; stir-fry gingerroot and garlic for 10 seconds. Add orange rind and red pepper; stir-fry for 1 minute or until red pepper is tender-crisp. Stir in soy sauce mixture; cook, stirring, until thickened.

• Return chicken to wok and stir until heated through. Makes 2 servings.

Chicken and Red Pepper Stir-Fry

STIR-FRIED CHICKEN AND SNOW PEAS

Use a wok if you have one because you can toss ingredients together easily while cooking. Team this quick and easy stir-fry with rice or thin noodles and serve lichee nuts for dessert.

1 lb	boneless skinless chicken breasts	500 g
1/3 cup	soy sauce	75 mL
2 tbsp	cornstarch	25 mL
1/2 lb	snow peas	250 g
	Vegetable oil	
1 tbsp	minced gingerroot	15 mL
	Salt and pepper	

• Dice chicken into 1-inch (2.5 cm) cubes and place in bowl. Combine 2 tbsp (25 mL) water, 2 tbsp (25 mL) of the soy sauce and 1 tbsp (15 mL) of the cornstarch; pour over chicken and marinate for 20 minutes.
• Combine 1/4 cup (50 mL) water, remaining soy sauce and cornstarch; set aside. Trim and halve peas; set aside.
• In wok or large skillet, heat 3 tbsp (50 mL) oil over high heat; cook chicken, stirring constantly, for 5 minutes. Remove from wok and set aside. Drain wok and wipe dry with paper towels.
• Heat another 3 tbsp (50 mL) oil in wok; cook ginger until fragrant but not browned. Add snow peas and stir to coat. Stir reserved soy sauce mixture and pour into wok; bring to boil, stirring. Add chicken and cook for 3 to 4 minutes or until heated through. Season with salt and pepper to taste. Makes about 4 servings.

SAUCY CHICKEN WITH GREEN ONIONS

Green onions add color and flavor to these chicken breasts. Serve with rice along with buttered carrots with ginger or herbs.

2 tbsp	(approx) butter	25 mL
4 to 6	boneless skinless chicken breasts (1 to 1-1/4 lb/500 to 625 g total)	4 to 6
1	bunch green onions (about 5), cut in 1-inch (2.5 cm) pieces	1
1	large clove garlic, minced	1
1 tbsp	all-purpose flour	15 mL
1/2 cup	chicken stock	125 mL
2 tbsp	whipping cream (optional)	25 mL
Pinch	ground allspice	Pinch
	Salt and pepper	

• In heavy skillet, melt butter over high heat; cook chicken breasts until browned, about 3 minutes on each side.
• Reduce heat to medium and add more butter, if necessary. Add green onions and garlic; cook for about 1 minute or until garlic is softened. Sprinkle with flour. Stir in stock and cook until slightly thickened and chicken is no longer pink inside, about 5 minutes.*
• Stir in cream (if using), allspice, and salt and pepper to taste. Makes 4 to 6 servings.
*If using bone-in chicken, cover and cook chicken in stock for 15 minutes or until chicken is no longer pink, adding more stock if necessary.

STIR-FRYING

You'll find stir-frying one of the speediest techniques for easy rush-hour meals. The combinations of ingredients are endless. Follow these simple tips for best results.

• **Read the recipe instructions carefully before you begin. Prepare the ingredients; combine the ones that go into the wok or skillet together. Set the ingredients out in small bowls or on waxed paper on a tray by the stove in the order you'll be using them.**
• **Cut each ingredient in pieces as uniform as possible in shape and size, for even cooking. Food cut in small pieces will cook more quickly and retain its flavor and texture.**
• **Stir-fry over the highest possible heat.**
• **Pay attention to cooking times and tests for doneness— the high heat will have the food cooked in seconds. As a general rule, undercook everything.**

Chicken Hash

CHICKEN HASH

Speed up cooking time even more by using leftovers of cooked chicken or ham and diced cooked potatoes. Just cook them until heated through before adding the peas and corn. You can omit the fried eggs if desired, but when the yolks break, they act as a sauce to moisten this colorful hash.

4	slices bacon, diced	4
1	onion, diced	1
2	cloves garlic, minced	2
2	boneless skinless chicken breasts (about 3/4 lb/ 375 g total), diced	2
2	large potatoes, peeled and diced	2
1 tbsp	vegetable oil	15 mL
1/2 cup	frozen peas	125 mL
1/2 cup	frozen corn kernels	125 mL
2 tbsp	chopped fresh parsley	25 mL
	Salt and pepper	
2 tbsp	butter	25 mL
4	eggs	4

• In large skillet, cook bacon over medium-high heat for 5 to 6 minutes or until crisp. Pour off fat, reserving 3 tbsp (50 mL) in skillet.

• Add onion and garlic to skillet; cook, stirring occasionally, for 2 minutes or until tender and fragrant.

• Add chicken, potatoes and oil to skillet; stir to coat well. Cover and cook for 5 minutes; stir. Cover and cook for 5 minutes longer or until potatoes are cooked through. Stir in peas and corn; cook, uncovered, for 5 minutes. Add parsley, and salt and pepper to taste. Divide among 4 plates; keep warm.

• In same skillet, melt butter over medium heat; cook eggs until whites are set but yolks are still runny. Place one egg over each serving of hash; season with salt and pepper to taste. Makes 4 servings.

SUCCOTASH STEW

Most meat departments sell packages of small drumsticks, which cook quickly in this vegetable stew. Serve with a tossed green salad, then follow with raspberry sherbet and sugar cookies for dessert.

6	slices bacon	6
8	small chicken drumsticks (1 to 1-1/2 lb/500 to 750 g total)	8
3	leeks (white and light green parts only), thickly sliced	3
1	can (12 oz/ 341 mL) corn kernels	1
1	pkg (10 oz/283 g) frozen lima beans	1
1 cup	chicken stock	250 mL
	Pepper	

• In skillet over medium heat, cook bacon, turning once, for 3 to 4 minutes or until crisp. Remove and drain on paper towels.
• In same pan, lightly brown chicken on all sides, 8 to 10 minutes. Add leeks to pan and cook for 3 to 4 minutes or until limp.
• Stir in corn, beans and stock. Season with pepper to taste. Bring to boil; reduce heat, cover and simmer for 20 minutes or until chicken is tender.
• Uncover and simmer for about 10 minutes longer or until stock is reduced and mixture is thickened slightly. Crumble bacon and sprinkle over stew. Makes 4 servings.

CHICKEN BREASTS PICCATA

This tart "lemony" preparation for chicken is quick and easy to make. It is also very versatile—inexpensive enough for an everyday meal but sophisticated enough for any dinner party.

4	large chicken breasts, skinned and boned	4
	Salt and pepper	
	All-purpose flour	
1/4 cup	unsalted butter	50 mL
1/2 cup	dry white wine	125 mL
1/3 cup	lemon juice	75 mL
2 tbsp	chopped fresh parsley and/or 3 tbsp (50 mL) chopped fresh dill	25 mL
2 tbsp	unsalted butter (optional)	25 mL
GARNISH:		
1	lemon, thinly sliced	1
	Parsley sprigs	

• Season chicken lightly with salt and pepper; dust lightly with flour.
• In skillet, melt 1/4 cup (50 mL) butter over medium-high heat until foaming; reduce heat slightly and cook chicken for about 7 minutes on each side or just until no longer pink inside.
• Remove chicken to serving platter and keep warm in 200°F (100°C) oven.
• Discard any excess fat in pan; add wine, lemon juice and parsley. Cook over medium-high heat, stirring constantly, for 2 to 3 minutes or until thickened. Remove from heat and stir in 2 tbsp (25 mL) butter if desired. Season with salt and pepper to taste. Pour over chicken. Garnish with lemon slices and parsley. Makes 4 servings.

Succotash Stew

POACHED TURKEY BREAST WITH LEMON CREAM SAUCE

Poached Turkey Breast
with Lemon Cream
Sauce

A simple green bean and red pepper salad makes a colorful accompaniment to this lovely turkey dish.

1-1/2 cups	chicken stock	375 mL
3/4 cup	dry white wine	175 mL
1/4 tsp	dried thyme	1 mL
1/4 tsp	black peppercorns	1 mL
1-1/4 lb	boneless skinless turkey breast	625 g
SAUCE:		
2 tbsp	butter	25 mL
1	small clove garlic, minced	1
2 tbsp	all-purpose flour	25 mL
3/4 cup	light cream	175 mL
2 tsp	grated lemon rind	10 mL
2 tbsp	lemon juice	25 mL
GARNISH:		
1 tsp	capers	5 mL

• In deep skillet or Dutch oven, combine stock, wine, thyme and peppercorns; cover and bring to boil. Add turkey breast and reduce heat to medium-low; poach gently, covered, for 20 to 30 minutes or until juices run clear when turkey is pierced with fork, turning breast over halfway through cooking. Strain cooking liquid, reserving 1/2 cup (125 mL). Transfer turkey to platter and cover loosely to keep warm while preparing sauce.

• **Sauce:** In small heavy saucepan, heat butter over medium heat; cook garlic until fragrant, about 1 minute. Add flour; cook, stirring, for 1 minute. Gradually whisk in reserved cooking liquid until smooth. Whisk in cream and any accumulated turkey juices from platter. Increase heat to medium-high and cook, whisking, for 2 to 3 minutes or until sauce comes to boil and is thick enough to coat spoon. Stir in lemon rind and juice.

• Slice turkey thinly and arrange overlapping slices on platter. Spoon some of the sauce over turkey; sprinkle with capers. Pass remaining sauce separately. Makes about 4 servings.

CHICKEN BREASTS WITH CHÈVRE AND JULIENNE PEPPERS

The red and green colors in this dish make a colorful complement to the goat cheese. You can easily double the recipe to serve four.

2	large chicken breasts, skinned and boned	2
	Salt and pepper	
1/2 cup	all-purpose flour	125 mL
1/4 cup	unsalted butter	50 mL
1	clove garlic, minced	1
1	each sweet red and green pepper, julienned	1
1/2 cup	dry white wine	125 mL
3 oz	fresh chèvre (semisoft goat cheese)	100 g

• Pat chicken dry with paper towels. Season lightly with salt and pepper; dust lightly with flour.

• In heavy skillet, melt 2 tbsp (25 mL) of the butter; cook chicken for 5 to 6 minutes on each side or just until cooked through and no longer pink inside.

• Meanwhile, in separate skillet, melt remaining butter; cook garlic and red and green peppers until fragrant and tender. With slotted spoon, transfer peppers to baking dish; place chicken on top.

• Discard any excess fat from skillet chicken was in. Pour in wine and cook, stirring, until reduced to a few tablespoons; pour over chicken. Crumble chèvre and sprinkle over chicken. Bake in 400°F (200°C) oven for 5 to 7 minutes or just until cheese begins to melt. Makes 2 servings.

Turkey and chicken cutlets: Use boneless skinless breasts. Slice a fresh turkey breast on the diagonal into cutlets and freeze what you don't use for another time. Tiny chicken breasts can be pounded to desired thickness without slicing.

TURKEY CUTLETS WITH LEMON AND ROSEMARY

Turkey cutlets taste similar to veal but are far less expensive. Accompany this dish with a Savory Vegetable Ring (recipe, p. 144) which can be finished in the oven while the cutlets cook.

1-1/2 lb	thin turkey cutlets	750 g
	Salt and pepper	
1 cup	all-purpose flour	250 mL
1/4 cup	unsalted butter	50 mL
1/2 cup	dry white wine or chicken stock	125 mL
1/4 cup	lemon juice	50 mL
1 tbsp	chopped fresh rosemary (or 1/2 tsp/2 mL dried)	15 mL
2 tbsp	unsalted butter	25 mL
1 tbsp	chopped fresh parsley	15 mL

• Pat turkey dry with paper towels; season lightly with salt and pepper; dredge with flour.

• In large skillet, heat 1/4 cup (50 mL) butter over medium-high heat; cook turkey, in batches if necessary, for about 4 minutes on each side or until lightly browned and just cooked through. Remove to serving platter and keep warm in 200°F (100°C) oven.

• Discard any excess fat from pan and add wine, lemon juice and rosemary; cook over medium-high heat, stirring, until reduced to about 1/4 cup (50 mL). Remove from heat; stir in 2 tbsp (25 mL) butter and parsley until butter is melted. Pour over turkey. Makes 6 servings.

Fish and Seafood

Fish and seafood are perfect for rush hour. Everyday meals can be super quick or even calorie trimmed with fish. Perk up family fare with Oriental Fish Fillets, Scallops and Broccoli with Almonds, or Lemon Shrimp with Fresh Vegetables. Raid the pantry for on-hand staple ingredients that require minimal preparation to dress up fish dishes. And get out the canned salmon or tuna for a simple supper like Baked Salmon Salad. Fish is fast. . .thank goodness you don't have time to overcook it!

ORIENTAL FISH FILLETS

Serve a bright vegetable and steamed rice with this zesty fish dish.

1 lb	frozen fish fillets (perch, sole or haddock), thawed	500 g
1/2 cup	orange juice	125 mL
2 tbsp	teriyaki or soy sauce	25 mL
1 tsp	minced gingerroot	5 mL
1 tsp	granulated sugar	5 mL
1	clove garlic, minced	1
Dash	hot pepper sauce	Dash
1 tsp	cornstarch	5 mL
1 tbsp	water	15 mL
1 tbsp	julienne orange rind	15 mL

• In large skillet, arrange fish in single layer. Combine orange juice, teriyaki sauce, ginger, sugar, garlic and hot pepper sauce; pour over fish. Bring to boil; reduce heat to simmer and cook, covered, for 3 to 5 minutes or until fish is opaque and flakes easily when tested with fork.

• Remove fish to serving platter, reserving orange juice mixture in skillet. Dissolve cornstarch in water; add to skillet. Bring to boil, stirring until thickened and smooth. Stir in orange rind. Pour sauce over fish. Makes 4 servings.

• **Microwave Directions:** In 9-inch (23 cm) pie plate, arrange fish fillets in circle with thin ends tucked under. Reduce orange juice to 1/3 cup (75 mL) and combine with teriyaki sauce, ginger, sugar, garlic and hot pepper sauce; pour over fish. Cover with vented plastic wrap and microwave at High for 4 to 5 minutes or until fish is opaque and flakes easily when tested with fork, rotating dish once during cooking time. Let stand, covered, for 5 minutes.

• With slotted spoon, remove fish to serving platter; pour orange juice mixture into 2-cup (500 mL) measure. Mix together cornstarch and water until smooth; stir into orange juice. Microwave at High for 1 minute or until thickened, stirring once during cooking. Stir in orange rind. Pour over fish.

Oriental Fish Fillets

FISH FILLETS IN PACKETS

Cooking in foil seals in flavor and juices. It's also handy for busy families; the fish can be prepared at once in individual packages and cooked individually as needed.

2 tbsp	butter	25 mL
1 lb	bluefish or other fish fillets, cut in serving-sized portions	500 g
1 cup	sliced mushrooms (optional)	250 mL
1/4 cup	chopped fresh parsley or dill (or 1 tsp/5 mL dried)	50 mL
4 tsp	lemon juice	20 mL
	Salt and pepper	

• Lightly butter 3 or 4 pieces of foil large enough to wrap fish. Place fish on buttered surface. Sprinkle with mushrooms (if using), parsley, lemon juice, and salt and pepper to taste; dot with remaining butter.
• Fold up foil to form loose packet; crimp edges to seal. Place on baking sheet and bake in 450°F (230°C) oven for 15 minutes or until fish is opaque and flakes easily when tested with fork. Place 1 packet on each plate and let diners open their own. Makes 3 or 4 servings.

SALMON PAT-A-CAKES WITH QUICK TARTAR SAUCE

These nutritious salmon cakes are crispy on the outside and soft on the inside.

2	large baking potatoes	2
1	can (7.5 oz/ 213 g) salmon	1
1/4 cup	chopped onion	50 mL
2 tbsp	chopped fresh parsley	25 mL
	Salt and pepper	
1/4 cup	dry bread crumbs	50 mL
2 tbsp	butter	25 mL
QUICK TARTAR SAUCE:		
1/3 cup	mayonnaise	75 mL
2 tbsp	chopped pickle	25 mL

• Peel potatoes and cut into small pieces. Boil for 10 minutes or until tender. Drain and mash.
• Drain salmon; stir into mashed potatoes. Add onion, parsley, and salt and pepper to taste. Mix well.
• Using hands, shape salmon mixture into 4 patties, about 1 inch (2.5 cm) thick and 3 inches (8 cm) in diameter. Press each patty into bread crumbs to coat.
• In large skillet, melt butter over medium-high heat; cook patties for about 3 minutes on each side or until golden and slightly crispy.
• **Quick Tartar Sauce:** Mix together mayonnaise and pickle; serve with patties. Makes 4 servings.

When you plan a meal around Salmon Pat-a-Cakes with Quick Tartar Sauce, serve lettuce wedges drizzled with an easy tomato dressing (2 tbsp/25 mL ketchup blended into 1/2 cup/ 125 mL mayonnaise) and a side dish of green or snow peas. For dessert, offer fresh fruit and vanilla wafers.

Oven-Poached Salmon in Dill Sauce

OVEN-POACHED SALMON IN DILL SAUCE

Salmon fillets stay moist and delicious when they are quickly oven-poached with wine. The fresh dill sauce is very easily made with poaching liquid, mayonnaise and yogurt. To reduce calories and fat, use light mayonnaise and low-fat yogurt.

1-1/2 lb	salmon fillets or steaks	750 g
	Salt and pepper	
1/4 cup	dry white wine	50 mL
1/3 cup	mayonnaise	75 mL
1/3 cup	plain yogurt	75 mL
1 tbsp	lemon juice	15 mL
2 tbsp	chopped fresh dill	25 mL

• Remove skin from salmon if using fillets. Cut fillets into serving-sized pieces; season lightly with salt and pepper to taste. Arrange in single layer in greased shallow baking dish; pour wine over. Cover and bake in 450°F (230°C) oven for 10 minutes per inch (2.5 cm) of thickness or until salmon is opaque. Carefully drain cooking liquid into small saucepan. Keep salmon warm while preparing sauce.

• Stir mayonnaise, yogurt and lemon juice into liquid in saucepan; heat over low heat just until warmed through (do not boil). Stir in dill and season with salt and pepper to taste. Spoon over salmon and serve immediately. Makes 4 to 6 servings.

Fish and Seafood 111

ALMOND-BREADED FILLETS

Rockfish is a popular Bermuda fish sometimes available in Canada; use it or any fresh white fillets such as sole, haddock or cod.

1/2 cup	unblanched almonds	125 mL
1/2 cup	fresh bread crumbs	125 mL
1	egg, lightly beaten	1
1/3 cup	milk	75 mL
1-1/4 lb	rockfish or other white fillets	625 g
3 tbsp	butter	50 mL
	Salt and pepper	
	Toasted sliced almonds	

• In food processor or blender, chop nuts finely; spread on plate or waxed paper. Toss with bread crumbs. Mix together egg and milk. Dip each fillet into milk mixture; press into nut and crumb mixture to coat.

• In heavy skillet, melt butter over medium-high heat until foamy; cook fillets for 3 to 4 minutes on each side or until golden on outside and fish flakes easily when tested with fork. Sprinkle with salt and pepper to taste. Garnish with toasted almond slices. Makes 4 or 5 servings.

Almond-Breaded Fillets

SOLE WITH BLACK BUTTER

Black butter or beurre noir *is traditional with skate, a flat ocean fish, but it's delicious with almost any fish.*

1 lb	**sole fillets**	**500 g**
	All-purpose flour, salt and pepper	
2 tbsp	**butter**	**25 mL**
BLACK BUTTER SAUCE:		
3 tbsp	**butter**	**50 mL**
1 tbsp	**white wine vinegar**	**15 mL**
1 tbsp	**chopped fresh parsley**	**15 mL**

• Lightly coat fillets with flour seasoned with salt and pepper. In heavy skillet, melt butter over medium-high heat; sauté fillets for 2 to 3 minutes on each side or until fish is opaque and flakes easily when tested with fork.

• **Black Butter Sauce:** In small heavy skillet or saucepan, heat butter over high heat until light brown. (Watch carefully; butter can quickly turn from brown to burnt.) Remove from heat and add vinegar and parsley; swirl pan to mix. Pour over fillets. Makes 4 servings.

FILLET OF SOLE WITH GREEN GRAPES

Serve this appealing dish with rice and steamed fresh vegetables.

2 lb	**sole fillets**	**1 kg**
2	**shallots (or 1 small onion), diced**	**2**
1/2 cup	**white wine**	**125 mL**
1/2 cup	**water**	**125 mL**
1 cup	**seedless green grapes, halved**	**250 mL**
SAUCE:		
1/2 cup	**whipping cream**	**125 mL**
1	**egg**	**1**
2 tbsp	**butter**	**25 mL**

• Sprinkle fillets with shallots; roll up and secure with toothpicks. Place in 13- x 9-inch (3.5 L) greased baking dish. Combine wine with water; pour over fish and cover with greased foil. Bake in 375°F (190°C) oven for 12 to 15 minutes or just until fish is opaque and flakes easily when tested with fork.

• **Sauce:** Meanwhile, in small saucepan, combine whipping cream, egg and butter; cook, whisking constantly, over medium-low heat for 5 minutes or until thick enough to coat back of spoon. Remove from heat.

• With slotted spoon, transfer fillets to shallow ovenproof dish; remove toothpicks. Scatter grapes over top; pour sauce over and broil for 3 to 4 minutes or until top is golden. Makes about 6 servings.

BAKED HADDOCK FILLETS WITH CHEESE

If you are using frozen fish fillets, thaw them completely to ensure even cooking.

1 cup	**shredded Cheddar cheese**	**250 mL**
2/3 cup	**fresh bread crumbs**	**150 mL**
1/2 tsp	**grated lemon rind**	**2 mL**
1/2 tsp	**dried basil**	**2 mL**
1/4 tsp	**dry mustard**	**1 mL**
Pinch	**nutmeg**	**Pinch**
	Salt and pepper	
2 tbsp	**butter, softened**	**25 mL**
1 lb	**haddock fillets**	**500 g**

• Combine 1/2 cup (125 mL) of the cheese with bread crumbs, lemon rind, basil, mustard, nutmeg, and salt and pepper to taste. Set aside.

• Grease 8-inch (2 L) square baking dish with 1 tbsp (15 mL) of the butter; sprinkle with half of the bread crumb mixture. Pat fillets dry with paper towels; arrange in baking dish and dot with remaining butter. Sprinkle remaining cheese over fish and top with remaining bread crumb mixture.

• Bake in 450°F (230°C) oven for 10 minutes per inch (5 to 7 minutes per cm) of thickness or until fish flakes easily when tested with fork. Makes 4 servings.

FISH FILLETS WITH LIME-GINGER SAUCE

Here's an easy way to serve any white fish, such as sole, halibut or orange roughy. The sauce takes only minutes to prepare and adds a wonderful piquant flavor to the fish.

1 lb	fish fillets (thawed if frozen)	500 g
LIME-GINGER SAUCE:		
1/3 cup	coarsely chopped gingerroot	75 mL
3	large green onions, coarsely chopped	3
1/3 cup	butter	75 mL
1 tbsp	grated lime rind	15 mL
1 tbsp	lime juice	15 mL
	Pepper	

• **Lime-Ginger Sauce:** In food processor, process ginger until finely chopped. Add onions, butter, lime rind and juice, and pepper to taste; process until smooth. Transfer to small saucepan; cook over low heat for 5 minutes.
• Place fish on lightly greased baking sheet; brush with butter mixture. Broil 4 inches (10 cm) from heat until sauce is bubbly and fish flakes easily when tested with fork, about 10 minutes per inch (2.5 cm) of thickness. Makes 4 servings.

BAKED WHITEFISH WITH MUSTARD-DILL SAUCE

Here's a quick yet elegant presentation for whitefish. Serve it with peas and a rice pilaf.

1	whitefish, cleaned (2-1/2 lb/ 1.25 kg)	1
1/2 tsp	salt	2 mL
1/2 tsp	pepper	2 mL
1	lemon, sliced	1
2	green onions, chopped	2
1/4 cup	chopped fresh dill	50 mL
1/4 cup	(approx) dry white wine	50 mL
2 tbsp	butter, melted	25 mL
MUSTARD-DILL SAUCE:		
2/3 cup	light cream	150 mL
1 tbsp	cornstarch	15 mL
1 tbsp	water	15 mL
1 tbsp	chopped fresh dill	15 mL
2 tsp	Dijon mustard	10 mL
	Salt and pepper	

• Remove fish head, and tail (if desired). Pat fish dry inside and out. Sprinkle cavity with salt and pepper. Arrange half of the lemon slices inside fish. Sprinkle green onions and dill over lemon; cover with remaining lemon slices.
• Place stuffed fish in large greased baking dish. Sprinkle with wine and brush with melted butter. Bake in 450°F (230°C) oven, allowing 10 minutes cooking time per inch (2.5 cm) of stuffed thickness (measure at centre of fish) or until fish is opaque and flakes easily when tested with fork near backbone. Drain off juices, adding more white wine, if necessary, to measure 1/3 cup (75 mL); set aside. Cover and keep fish warm.
• **Mustard-Dill Sauce:** In small saucepan, bring cream to boil. Dissolve cornstarch in water; whisk into cream and cook, whisking, until thickened and smooth. Stir in reserved fish juices, dill and mustard. Season with salt and pepper to taste. Serve with fish. Makes 4 to 6 servings.
• **Microwave Directions:** Place stuffed fish on microwaveable serving platter; cover with vented plastic wrap. Microwave at High for 7 to 11 minutes or until fish is opaque and flakes easily when tested with fork near backbone, rotating platter twice during cooking. Drain off juices, adding more white wine, if necessary, to measure 1/3 cup (75 mL); set aside. Let fish stand, covered, for 5 minutes.

COOKING FISH

Because fish is naturally tender (does not have any connective tissue), it takes very little time to cook. A simple but reliable method to estimate the cooking time of fish in a hot oven (450°F/230°C) is to allow 10 minutes for every inch (2.5 cm) of thickness of fresh fish (double the time if frozen) measured at the thickest point. Fish is done when the flesh is opaque and flakes easily when tested with a fork.

Baked Whitefish with Mustard-Dill Sauce

LEMON SHRIMP WITH FRESH VEGETABLES

Asparagus, cucumbers and tomatoes are very tender vegetables with sweet fresh flavor, especially when cooked oriental style. To make Lemon Chicken, substitute cubes or strips of chicken breast for the shrimp.

1/2 lb	fresh asparagus	250 g
1	onion	1
2	tomatoes	2
1	seedless cucumber	1
1 lb	shrimp	500 g
1/4 cup	peanut or vegetable oil	50 mL
2 tbsp	water	25 mL
	Salt	
2	slices gingerroot	2
8	slices lemon	8

LEMON SAUCE:

3/4 cup	granulated sugar	175 mL
1 tbsp	cornstarch	15 mL
1/2 cup	water	125 mL
1/4 cup	lemon juice	50 mL
2 tbsp	vinegar	25 mL
	Salt	
	Yellow food coloring (optional)	

• Cut asparagus diagonally into 2-inch (5 cm) long pieces. Cut onion and tomatoes into wedges. Cut cucumber in half lengthwise, then into 1/4-inch (5 mm) chunks. Peel and devein shrimp.

• **Lemon Sauce:** In saucepan, combine sugar and cornstarch; mix in water, lemon juice and vinegar. Bring to boil, stirring; cook for 1 to 2 minutes or until thickened. Season with salt to taste; add a few drops yellow food coloring if desired. Keep warm.

• Meanwhile, in large skillet or wok, heat 2 tbsp (25 mL) of the oil. Add asparagus and stir-fry for 1 minute. Add water and sprinkle lightly with salt to taste; cover and steam until asparagus is nearly tender, about 2 minutes. Remove asparagus and set aside. Drain skillet.

• Add remaining oil to skillet and stir-fry onion and ginger for about 4 minutes or until tender. Remove ginger. Add shrimp and stir-fry for 2 minutes. Add cucumber, tomatoes and asparagus; cover and steam for 2 to 3 minutes or just until asparagus is tender-crisp and shrimp are pink. Taste and adjust seasoning.

• Stir in lemon sauce and lemon slices; bring to boil, stirring gently. Serve immediately. Makes 4 servings.

SCALLOPS AND BROCCOLI WITH ALMONDS

This makes a delightful meal for two, or you can double it for four. Assemble all ingredients before you start cooking. That way it takes less than 10 minutes to cook supper. Serve with raw vegetable sticks and steamed rice. For an after-dinner treat, serve fortune cookies and green tea.

1/2 lb	scallops	250 g
1	bunch broccoli (about 1/2 lb/ 250 g)	1
4	green onions	4
1	slice gingerroot (about 1/4 inch/ 5 mm thick)	1
1/4 cup	chicken stock or water	50 mL
1 tbsp	dry sherry	15 mL
1 tbsp	light soy sauce	15 mL
1 tsp	cornstarch	5 mL
1/2 tsp	granulated sugar	2 mL
2 tbsp	(approx) vegetable oil	25 mL
	Pepper	
1/4 cup	toasted sliced almonds* (optional)	50 mL

- Rinse scallops under cold water; pat dry with paper towels. Separate broccoli into bite-sized florets; cut stalks thinly on diagonal. Chop green onions and gingerroot. In bowl, blend together chicken stock, sherry, soy sauce, cornstarch and sugar.
- In wok or heavy skillet, heat oil over high heat until hot but not smoking. Stir-fry scallops, turning constantly, just until scallops are opaque, about 2 minutes. Remove with slotted spoon to serving dish and keep warm.
- If necessary, add more oil to wok. Add broccoli, green onions and gingerroot; stir until coated with oil. Stir in chicken stock mixture to coat vegetables well; cover and steam for 2 minutes or until vegetables are tender-crisp and sauce thickens.
- Return scallops to wok and toss to coat. Season with pepper to taste. Serve immediately, sprinkled with almonds (if using). Makes 2 servings.
*Toast almonds on baking sheet in 350°F (180°C) oven for 5 minutes or until golden, or cook quickly in 1 tsp (5 mL) butter in small skillet over medium-high heat.

Make your own croutons for Baked Salmon Salad or any other salad. Quickly stir-fry 1 cup (250 mL) small bread cubes in 1 tbsp (15 mL) melted butter until golden and crisp. Variations:
- *Garlic—add 1 minced garlic clove to melted butter.*
- *Parmesan—toss croutons with 1 tbsp (15 mL) Parmesan cheese just before removing from skillet.*
- *Herbed—add 1/2 tsp (2 mL) of your favorite dried herb (basil, oregano, thyme, etc.) to melted butter.*

BAKED SALMON SALAD

Spoon the hot salad into lettuce cups after baking and serve with toasted chunks of crusty bread.

1	can (7.5 oz/ 213 g) salmon, drained	1
1-1/2 cups	peas (frozen or canned)	375 mL
1 cup	croutons	250 mL
1/2 cup	mayonnaise	125 mL
1/2 cup	diced sweet green pepper	125 mL
1/2 cup	diced celery	125 mL
1/4 cup	chili sauce	50 mL
2 tbsp	freshly grated Parmesan cheese	25 mL
	Lettuce	

- Combine salmon, peas, croutons, mayonnaise, green pepper, celery and chili sauce; toss lightly to combine.
- Spoon into greased 4-cup (1 L) casserole; sprinkle with Parmesan. Bake in 350°F (180°C) oven for 20 minutes or until heated through. Spoon into lettuce cups and serve at once. Makes 4 main-dish servings or 6 appetizer servings.
- **Microwave Directions:** Prepare as directed, spooning into 4 scallop shells or individual dishes. Microwave, covered loosely with waxed paper, at High for 2 minutes. Rearrange dishes and microwave at Medium-High (70%) for another 2 to 4 minutes longer or until heated through. Let stand for 5 minutes.

ORIENTAL HOT POT

This cook-it-yourself meal is great fun for guests. When you're really in a hurry, you can eliminate some of the vegetables.

1/2 lb	each boneless chicken breasts, beef tenderloin, pork tenderloin and medium shrimp	250 g
1/2 lb	tofu, cut in small squares	250 g
3/4 lb	broccoli, cut in florets	375 g
1	small head cauliflower, cut in florets	1
1/2 lb	snow peas, trimmed	250 g
1/2 lb	fresh mushrooms, cut in half	250 g
4	carrots, peeled and thinly sliced	4
4	stalks celery, thinly sliced	4
4	green onions, thinly sliced	4
10 cups	(approx) chicken stock	2.5 L
2 tbsp	soy sauce	25 mL
1 tbsp	sherry	15 mL
2	dashes hot pepper sauce	2
1/2 lb	cellophane noodles or rice vermicelli	250 g

CONDIMENTS:

	Ginger Chutney Sauce (sidebar, opposite page)
	Plum sauce
	Teriyaki sauce
	Mustard

• Cut chicken, beef and pork into very thin strips; peel and devein shrimp. Arrange chicken, meat, shrimp and tofu on large platter. Arrange broccoli, cauliflower, snow peas, mushrooms, carrots, celery and onions on 1 or 2 other platters.

• Pour stock into 2 stainless steel or enamelled fondue pots, using enough to fill each pot about two-thirds full. To each pot, add half of the soy sauce, half of the sherry and half of the hot pepper sauce; bring to boil.

• Transfer pots to table and set each over a spirit burner; return to boil. Surround with platters of meat, vegetables and small bowls of condiments.

• Have guests spear chicken, meat, shrimp and tofu on fondue forks and immerse in boiling stock until cooked, 1 to 2 minutes.

• Add assortment of vegetables to pot and remove with slotted spoon when cooked, 3 to 4 minutes. Dip cooked food into choice of condiment.

• When fondue foods are finished, add cellophane noodles to stock. Cook for 4 to 5 minutes or until tender. Serve stock with noodles in small soup bowls or mugs. Makes 4 to 6 servings.

SCALLOPS PROVENÇALE

This tasty Provençale sauce is also delicious on salmon steaks and shrimp instead of scallops. Serve with rice or noodles.

2 tbsp	butter or vegetable oil	25 mL
2	cloves garlic, finely chopped	2
1	onion, finely chopped	1
5	tomatoes, peeled, seeded and chopped (or 1 can 28 oz/ 796 mL plum tomatoes, drained)	5
1/2 cup	dry white wine	125 mL
1/4 tsp	pepper	1 mL
1-1/2 lb	scallops	750 g
	Salt	
1/4 cup	chopped fresh parsley or basil	50 mL

• In skillet, heat butter; cook garlic and onion, without browning, until tender and fragrant. Add tomatoes; cook for a few minutes until any liquid has evaporated. Add wine and pepper; cook for about 5 minutes or until liquid is reduced by half.
• Add scallops and cook, stirring, for about 6 minutes or until just opaque and cooked through. Season with salt to taste; sprinkle with parsley. Serve immediately. Makes 6 servings.

GINGER CHUTNEY SAUCE

Serve this tasty condiment with the Oriental Hot Pot. In small saucepan, combine 1/2 cup (125 mL) chutney, 2 tbsp (25 mL) soy sauce and 1 tbsp (15 mL) grated gingerroot; bring to boil, mixing well. Remove from heat and serve. Makes about 3/4 cup (175 mL).

MUSSELS WITH GARLIC AND TOMATOES

Tasty mussels are quick and easy even when you're in a hurry. Serve this version as a main dish or as an appetizer. You can substitute clams for the mussels. Just increase the cooking time to 5 to 10 minutes.

2 lb	mussels	1 kg
2 tbsp	butter	25 mL
1/4 cup	finely chopped onion	50 mL
1	clove garlic, minced	1
Pinch	hot pepper flakes	Pinch
1/2 cup	dry white wine	125 mL
2	tomatoes, seeded and chopped	2
1 tbsp	olive oil	15 mL
1/4 cup	chopped fresh basil	50 mL
	Salt and pepper	

• Scrub mussels thoroughly; remove "beard" or hairlike bits. Discard any mussels that don't close when tapped.
• In large saucepan, melt butter over medium heat; cook onion, garlic and hot pepper flakes for about 2 minutes or until softened.
• Add wine; bring to boil. Add mussels; cover and steam for 4 to 6 minutes or until mussels open. Discard any that do not open. Remove from heat.
• Strain broth into separate saucepan; bring to boil and boil vigorously until liquid is reduced by about one-half.
• Stir in tomatoes; reduce heat to simmer. Blend in olive oil and half of the basil. Season with salt and pepper to taste. Pour sauce over mussels. Sprinkle with remaining basil. Makes 4 appetizers or 2 main-course servings.

Eggs and Cheese

Eggs are always great for breakfast or brunch, but with a little special treatment they make wonderful rush-hour main dishes. Try our dressed-up omelettes for an elegant presentation or a Spanish Tortilla for a heartier family supper. Discover some new twists to old favorites with recipes like Country Garden Poached Eggs and Light Eggs Benedict with Prosciutto. Cheese is also a marvelous convenience food, which you can use for a late-night meal like Cheddar-Soufflé Omelette. Or for instant nostalgia make Real Welsh Rarebit.

WATERCRESS FRITTATA

Enjoy this with chili sauce, toast triangles and a glass of white wine for a quick lunch, brunch or light after-theatre supper.

4	eggs	4
2	egg whites	2
1/3 cup	freshly grated Parmesan cheese	75 mL
1/2 tsp	salt	2 mL
Pinch	pepper	Pinch
1	bunch watercress	1
1 tbsp	olive oil	15 mL
1 cup	sliced mushrooms	250 mL
2	cloves garlic, minced	2
2	green onions, sliced	2
1/2 tsp	dried basil	2 mL
1/4 lb	mozzarella cheese, cut in thin strips	125 g

• In bowl, whisk together eggs, egg whites, 1/4 cup (50 mL) of the Parmesan, salt and pepper; set aside.
• Remove enough watercress leaves to measure 1 cup (250 mL) packed; discard stems and set remaining sprigs aside for garnish.
• In large ovenproof skillet, heat oil over medium-high heat; cook mushrooms, garlic, onions and basil until mushrooms are lightly browned, about 3 minutes. Add watercress; cook, stirring often, until leaves are wilted, about 2 minutes.
• Remove skillet from heat and stir in remaining Parmesan; spread evenly over bottom of skillet and pour egg mixture over top. Cook over medium heat for 1 minute; sprinkle with mozzarella and place skillet under broiler. Broil until cheese begins to brown, 2 to 3 minutes. Slide onto warm serving plate and cut into wedges to serve garnished with watercress sprigs. Makes 4 servings.

Watercress Frittata

FRITTATA IN A SKILLET

You can change the flavor of this frittata by varying the cheese and fruit. Swiss, Edam, Muenster or Jarlsberg cheese can be used instead of Cheddar. Peaches, plums or nectarines may be substituted for the apple. Serve with halved cherry tomatoes drizzled with a light vinaigrette (p.22).

2 tbsp	butter	25 mL
1	leek (white part only) or small onion, chopped	1
4	eggs	4
1/4 cup	plain yogurt	50 mL
1/2 tsp	salt	2 mL
1/4 tsp	hot pepper sauce	1 mL
1/3 cup	fresh bread crumbs	75 mL
1	small red apple (unpeeled)	1
1/2 cup	shredded Cheddar cheese	125 mL

• In skillet, melt butter over medium heat; add leek and cook for 4 minutes or until softened but not browned.
• Meanwhile, in small bowl, beat eggs until frothy. Blend in yogurt, salt and hot pepper sauce; stir in bread crumbs. Pour over leeks in skillet. Increase heat to medium-high and cook, covered, for 3 to 4 minutes or until almost set.
• Cut apple into cubes. Sprinkle over frittata; top with cheese. Cover and cook for 3 minutes or until cheese is melted.
• Remove from heat and let stand, covered, until top is set and apples are tender, about 3 minutes. Cut into wedges to serve. Makes about 4 servings.

BACON AND SWISS CHEESE FRITTATA

It's a pleasure to make a satisfying evening meal out of basic ingredients. Substitute other cheeses such as Cheddar, Colby or Havarti if preferred. Serve with crusty onion rolls and a crunchy cabbage and carrot slaw.

8	slices lean bacon	8
2 tbsp	butter	25 mL
2 tbsp	chopped green onion	25 mL
6	eggs	6
1/2 tsp	salt	2 mL
Pinch	pepper	Pinch
1/4 cup	shredded Swiss cheese	50 mL
2 tbsp	freshly grated Parmesan cheese	25 mL

• In 10-inch (25 cm) ovenproof skillet, fry bacon until crisp; drain off fat. Remove bacon and pat dry with paper towels. Cut each strip in half and set aside. With paper towel, wipe skillet clean.
• In skillet, melt butter over medium heat; cook onion until softened, about 3 minutes. In bowl, beat eggs with salt and pepper; pour over onion. Cook until bottom sets, lifting frittata with spatula to allow uncooked eggs to flow underneath and set.
• When eggs are almost completely set, arrange bacon, pinwheel-fashion on top of frittata. Sprinkle with Swiss and Parmesan cheeses. Broil about 3 inches (7 cm) from heat until golden and set, about 3 minutes. Cut into wedges to serve. Makes 4 servings.

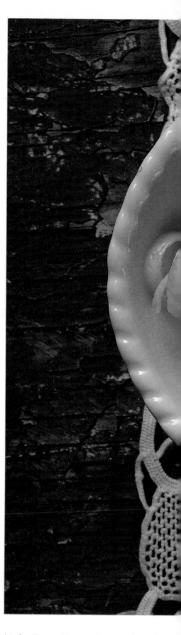

Light Eggs Benedict with Prosciutto

STORING EGGS

Eggs are perishable. Store them in your refrigerator, large ends up, in the container in which you bought them rather than on the refrigerator door where vibrations and temperature changes can affect them. Store eggs away from strong-smelling foods because they can absorb odors.

LIGHT EGGS BENEDICT WITH PROSCIUTTO

Prosciutto and a butterless Hollandaise make a lighter version of the classic brunch dish.

4	**English muffins or slices French bread**	4
2 tbsp	**unsalted butter**	25 mL
1/4 lb	**prosciutto, slivered or sliced**	125 g
8	**poached eggs**	8
LIGHT HOLLANDAISE SAUCE:		
3	**eggs**	3
3 tbsp	**lemon juice**	50 mL
1/4 cup	**hot water**	50 mL
1/4 tsp	**white pepper**	1 mL
Dash	**hot pepper sauce**	Dash

• **Light Hollandaise Sauce:** In large bowl, whisk together eggs, lemon juice and hot water. Place over pan of hot, not boiling, water and whisk until fluffy and thickened, 3 to 4 minutes. Whisk in pepper and hot pepper sauce; cover and keep warm over hot water for up to 30 minutes.

• Meanwhile, split muffins; toast and place on hot plates. Keep warm. In small skillet, melt butter; sauté prosciutto just until heated through. Place on top of muffins; top each with poached egg and spoon sauce over. Makes 4 servings.

SCRAMBLED EGGS WITH GREEN ONIONS

Scrambled Eggs with Green Onions

For creamier scrambled eggs, mix eggs with 2 tbsp (25 mL) milk and 2 tbsp (25 mL) sour cream instead of 1/4 cup (50 mL) milk.

8	eggs	8
1/4 cup	milk	50 mL
Pinch	each salt and cayenne pepper	Pinch
2	green onions, chopped	2
1 tbsp	butter	15 mL

• In large bowl, whisk together eggs, milk, salt, cayenne pepper and green onions. In skillet, heat butter over medium heat; cook egg mixture, stirring, for 4 to 6 minutes or until creamy and set. Makes about 4 servings.

VARIATIONS:

TOMATO, BASIL AND BACON:

6	slices crisp cooked bacon, chopped	6
1	tomato, seeded and diced	1
2 tbsp	chopped fresh basil	25 mL

• Add bacon to egg mixture in bowl. Cook as above until eggs are set. Sprinkle with tomato and basil.

CHEESE, MUSHROOM AND PEPPER:

1 tbsp	vegetable oil	15 mL
Half	sweet green pepper, chopped	Half
1 cup	sliced mushrooms	250 mL
1 cup	shredded Swiss cheese	250 mL
1/4 tsp	dried tarragon	1 mL

• In skillet, heat oil over medium-high heat and cook green pepper and mushrooms for 2 to 3 minutes or until softened; remove and set aside. Add cheese and tarragon to egg mixture in bowl. Cook eggs as above, stirring in cooked pepper and mushrooms just before eggs set.

Spanish Tortilla

COOK A PERFECT EGG

• **Fried: To avoid rubbery egg whites, cook eggs over medium-low heat, just until whites are set. Turn to cook other side, if desired.**

• **Hard-cooked: Eggs cooked in the shell should never be boiled. Pierce large ends to prevent cracking. Place eggs in saucepan and add enough water to come at least 1 inch (2.5 cm) above eggs. Bring to boil; remove from heat to prevent further boiling. Let eggs stand in hot water for 20 minutes. Drain and cool eggs immediately under cold running water.**

• **Microwave scrambled: In small bowl, microwave 1 tsp (5 mL) butter at High for 20 to 30 seconds or until melted. Using fork, blend in 2 eggs and 2 tbsp (25 mL) milk or water. Microwave at High for 1 to 1-1/2 minutes or until curds have formed but mixture is still creamy. Season with salt and pepper to taste.**

SPANISH TORTILLA

This quiche-like pie contains meat, cheese, vegetables and eggs, so it's a great meal-in-a-dish. Cut into smaller pieces, it also makes a wonderful appetizer. You can also top this with your favorite tomato sauce.

1/4 cup	butter or olive oil	50 mL
1	clove garlic, finely chopped	1
1	onion, finely chopped	1
1	sweet red pepper, diced	1
1	sweet green pepper, diced	1
1/2 lb	Polish sausage, sliced and cut in quarters	250 g
1/2 lb	potatoes, peeled, cooked and sliced	250 g
2 cups	shredded Swiss cheese	500 mL
6	eggs	6
1/3 cup	water	75 mL
1 tsp	salt	5 mL
1/4 tsp	black pepper	1 mL
Pinch	cayenne pepper	Pinch

• In large skillet, melt butter over medium heat; cook garlic and onion until softened but not browned. Add red and green peppers; cook for a few minutes longer or until tender. Let cool; transfer to buttered 10-inch (25 cm) pie plate or 8-cup (2 L) casserole dish.

• Add sausage, potatoes and cheese to vegetables in pie plate; stir gently to mix.

• Beat eggs with water, salt, black and cayenne peppers; pour over vegetable mixture. Bake in 350°F (180°C) oven for 30 to 35 minutes or until top is golden and centre feels firm when gently touched. Let stand for 10 minutes; cut into wedges or squares to serve. Makes 4 to 6 servings.

INDIVIDUAL THREE-CHEESE SOUFFLÉS

No sauce to make, no eggs to separate—
this has to be the easiest soufflé recipe
around. The cheesy custard mixture puffs
up just like a regular soufflé. The time
allotted for baking gives these soufflés a
typical soft creamy centre, but if you like a
soufflé that's firm throughout, bake for 5
minutes longer. Serve with a spinach salad
and crusty bread.

2	eggs	2
3 tbsp	light cream	50 mL
2 tbsp	freshly grated Parmesan cheese	25 mL
1/2 tsp	Dijon mustard	2 mL
Dash	hot pepper sauce	Dash
1/4 lb	sharp Cheddar cheese, cubed	125 g
1/4 lb	cream cheese, cubed	125 g

• Butter 4 individual 2/3-cup (150 mL) soufflé dishes or custard cups; set aside.
• In blender, combine eggs, cream, Parmesan, mustard and hot pepper sauce; blend until smooth.
• With motor running, add Cheddar, a few cubes at a time. Repeat with cream cheese until blended. Process at high speed for 5 seconds or until smooth and creamy.
• Pour mixture into prepared dishes. Bake in 375°F (190°C) oven for 15 minutes or until golden brown. Serve immediately. Makes 4 servings.

ROESTI POTATOES WITH POACHED EGGS

Roesti potatoes are thin, crisp grated
potato pancakes. Top them with poached
eggs and they make a simple but tasty
supper, especially when served with sliced
tomatoes and back bacon.

6	potatoes (about 2-1/2 lb/1.25 kg)	6
1/3 cup	butter, melted	75 mL
1 tsp	salt	5 mL
1/2 tsp	pepper	2 mL
4	eggs	4

• Peel and quarter potatoes. In saucepan, cover potatoes with cold salted water; cover and bring to boil. Cook for about 5 minutes or until partially cooked but still quite firm. Let cool enough to handle. Grate potatoes.
• In 11-inch (28 cm) skillet, preferably nonstick, heat half of the butter over medium-high heat until sizzling; tilt to coat surface of pan. Add potatoes and press into large flat pancake shape; sprinkle with salt and pepper.
• Using knife, loosen potatoes from edge of pan to make it easier to run spatula underneath. Cook for about 5 minutes or until bottom is golden brown. Using spatula, loosen pancake; slide onto large plate and drizzle remaining butter over uncooked side of pancake. Invert pancake back into skillet; cook for about 5 minutes or until underside is golden brown. Loosen and slide onto serving platter.
• Meanwhile, poach eggs; drain. Arrange on top of roesti potato pancake. Makes about 4 servings.

POACHED EGGS

• *Use the freshest eggs you can get. In saucepan, bring 4 cups (1 L) water and 2 tbsp (25 mL) vinegar to boil. Break 2 eggs into small bowl. Stir boiling water to create whirlpool effect and carefully slip eggs into centre. Reduce heat and simmer for 4 minutes or until eggs are soft-cooked. Serve immediately.*
• *Steam-poached in the microwave: Break 1 egg into buttered custard cup. Using toothpick, pierce yolk; cover with vented plastic wrap. Microwave at Medium-High (70%) for 45 to 60 seconds for 1 egg, 1 to 1-1/2 minutes for 2 eggs, 1-1/2 to 2 minutes for 3 eggs or until just set. Let stand for 1 to 2 minutes.*

*Country Garden
Poached Eggs*

COUNTRY GARDEN POACHED EGGS

*This simple yet special dish features
poached eggs floating on a nest of colorful
vegetables. Accompany with toasted
grainy bread or fresh crusty rolls.*

12	green beans	12
2	carrots	2
2	small zucchini	2
1	small sweet red pepper	1
2 cups	chicken stock	500 mL
2 tsp	lemon juice	10 mL
1 tsp	dried basil	5 mL
2 tbsp	cold butter	25 mL
2 tbsp	chopped fresh parsley	25 mL
4	hot poached eggs	4

• Cut beans into 1-inch (2.5 cm) lengths;
cut carrots, zucchini and red pepper into
sticks same size as beans.

• In saucepan, bring chicken stock to boil;
add beans and carrots and cook for 4
minutes. Add zucchini and red pepper;
cook for 5 minutes. With slotted spoon,
remove vegetables and divide among 4
warmed shallow soup bowls.

• Stir lemon juice and basil into saucepan;
whisk in butter one-third at a time. Stir in
parsley. Top each bowl of vegetables with
poached egg; pour broth over eggs. Serve
immediately. Makes 4 servings.

MOCK CHEESE SOUFFLÉ

This is really a savory bread-and-cheese pudding with a lovely golden crust. It's best made with Italian or French bread that is cut in 1/2-inch (1 cm) cubes and is great served with crisp green vegetables.

8 cups	day-old bread cubes	2 L
2 cups	shredded old Cheddar cheese	500 mL
1/4 tsp	pepper	1 mL
2 cups	milk	500 mL
2 tbsp	butter	25 mL
2 tsp	Dijon mustard	10 mL
5	eggs	5
1 tsp	salt	5 mL
Pinch	cayenne pepper	Pinch
1 tbsp	freshly grated Parmesan cheese	15 mL
	Watercress (optional)	

• In greased 9-inch (2.5 L) square baking dish, spread half of the bread. Sprinkle with half of the Cheddar; season with half of the pepper. Repeat layers with remaining bread, Cheddar and pepper.

• In small saucepan, warm milk and butter over medium heat until butter melts and little bubbles form around edge of pan. Blend in mustard.

• In large bowl, beat eggs; stir in milk mixture, salt and cayenne. Pour evenly over bread mixture; sprinkle with Parmesan. Let stand for 10 minutes to soften bread.

• Bake in 350°F (180°C) oven for 35 minutes or until top is crisp, golden and puffed. Garnish with watercress (if using). Makes 4 servings.

REAL WELSH RAREBIT

According to folklore, Welsh Rarebit (pronounced rabbit) was created by an ingenious cook from the ingredients she found in the larder after the master of the house failed to bag a rabbit for dinner that evening. Serve over cooked asparagus, broccoli, zucchini or green beans, or on toasted bread.

2 tbsp	butter	25 mL
1/4 cup	all-purpose flour	50 mL
1/2 tsp	dry mustard	2 mL
1	can (355 mL) ale or beer	1
1 tsp	Worcestershire sauce	5 mL
Dash	hot pepper sauce	Dash
3 cups	shredded old Cheddar cheese	750 mL

• In saucepan, melt butter over medium heat; stir in flour and mustard. Gradually stir in ale and bring to boil; cook, stirring, for 3 minutes or until thickened and smooth.

• Stir in Worcestershire and hot pepper sauce. Gradually add cheese, stirring briskly until cheese has melted. Immediately remove from heat. (Boiling can cause cheese to curdle.) Makes 4 to 6 servings.

If breakfast time is the rush hour at your house, serve leftovers of Real Welsh Rarebit, quickly reheated in the microwave and spooned over toasted English muffins. Add a glass of juice and a steaming cup of coffee or an ice cold glass of milk for a completely balanced breakfast— a perfect start to the day.

CHEDDAR-SOUFFLÉ OMELETTE

The secret of this puffy omelette is in the stiffly beaten egg whites. It's fun to see the omelette puff up in the pan; serve immediately while still gloriously risen. This is good with a cucumber and sour cream salad and warm croissants.

8	eggs, separated	8
2 tbsp	milk	25 mL
1 tsp	salt	5 mL
Pinch	pepper	Pinch
Dash	Worcestershire sauce	Dash
1/4 cup	butter	50 mL
1 cup	finely shredded old Cheddar cheese (about 4 oz/125 g)	250 mL

• In large bowl, beat egg whites until stiff but not dry peaks form.

• In small bowl, beat together egg yolks, milk, salt, pepper and Worcestershire sauce. Pour over egg whites and gently fold together.

• In deep ovenproof 10-inch (25 cm) skillet, melt butter over medium-low heat; pour in egg mixture. Sprinkle with cheese and cook for 5 to 8 minutes or until omelette has pulled away from side of skillet.

• Broil 4 inches (10 cm) from heat for 3 to 4 minutes or until omelette is puffed, cheese melts and top is golden. Serve immediately. Makes 5 or 6 servings.

Pasta, Rice and Grains

Super-quick dinners benefit from pasta power, whether as a side dish with a simple meat or as a meal in itself. Mix and match the endless pasta shapes with a variety of sauces to create new menu possibilities. Try Linguine with Fresh Tomatoes and Seafood or Gnocchi with Four Cheeses when you want a more elegant dish. And nutrition-conscious cooks will welcome our recipes using grains, today's highly-touted complex carbohydrates. Choose recipes for rice, barley, bulgur or couscous for a pleasant change of pace.

PASTA SHELLS WITH RED PEPPER AND PARSLEY SAUCE

Garlic and anchovies give this parsley sauce its rich flavor. Sautéed red peppers provide a colorful contrast to the green sauce.

1 cup	parsley leaves	250 mL
2	anchovies, rinsed	2
1	clove garlic	1
1/3 cup	olive oil	75 mL
1	sweet red pepper, thinly sliced	1
3/4 lb	pasta shells or bows	375 g
1/2 cup	freshly grated Parmesan cheese	125 mL
	Salt and pepper	

• In food processor or blender, combine parsley, anchovies and garlic; process until finely minced. With motor running, gradually add 1/4 cup (50 mL) of the oil; process until mixture forms a paste.
• In skillet, heat remaining oil over medium-high heat; sauté red pepper for 2 to 3 minutes or just until tender-crisp. Remove from heat.
• Meanwhile, in large pot of boiling salted water, cook pasta until al dente (tender but firm). Drain and add to skillet along with parsley sauce and cheese. Toss to mix. Season with salt and pepper to taste. Makes 4 servings.

Rotini with Salmon and Chives (p. 133); Pasta Shells with Red Pepper and Parsley Sauce

TOMATO LINGUINE WITH SALMON

Linguine with Smoked Salmon

Both fresh pasta and fish cook very quickly so you won't have to wait long for this colorful supper. Tomato linguine is available in the refrigerated section of most supermarkets. Specialty and gourmet food shops often stock both fresh and dried tomato linguine.

1/2 lb	salmon fillets or steaks	250 g
	Salt and pepper	
2 tbsp	vegetable oil	25 mL
2 tbsp	butter	25 mL
5	green onions, thinly sliced	5
2 tbsp	finely chopped fresh parsley	25 mL
1 tbsp	lemon juice	15 mL
3/4 lb	tomato linguine	375 g
1/2 cup	coarsely chopped watercress	125 mL

• Cut salmon into bite-sized pieces (remove skin and bones if using salmon steaks). Season with salt and pepper to taste.
• In large skillet, heat oil over medium heat; add salmon and cook for about 3 minutes or until opaque. Remove with slotted spoon to warm plate.
• Add butter to skillet, then onions and parsley; cook for 1 minute. Stir in lemon juice; return salmon to skillet and cook for 1 minute or until heated through.
• Meanwhile, in large pot of boiling salted water, cook linguine until al dente (tender but firm); drain. Add linguine and watercress to skillet; toss gently to coat linguine. Season with salt and a coarse grinding of pepper to taste. Makes about 4 servings.

LINGUINE WITH SMOKED SALMON:

3/4 lb	linguine	375 g
1/2 lb	smoked salmon	250 g
2 tbsp	butter	25 mL
5	green onions, julienned	5
2 tbsp	chopped fresh parsley	25 mL
1 tbsp	lemon juice	15 mL
1/2 cup	chopped watercress	125 mL
	Pepper	

• In pot of boiling salted water, cook linguine until al dente (tender but firm); drain.
• Meanwhile, cut salmon into strips. In skillet, melt butter over medium heat; cook salmon, onions, parsley and lemon juice for 1 minute or until heated through. Add linguine and watercress to skillet; toss gently to coat. Season with pepper to taste. Makes about 4 servings.

COOKING PASTA

• *Cook pasta in a large pot that allows plenty of room for the water to boil briskly and pasta to cook without being crowded.*
• *Bring water to a rolling boil; add salt, then add the pasta all at once. Bring back to boil. Stir to separate pasta and boil quickly.*
• *Cooking times vary depending on size and shape of pasta and whether it is fresh or dried. Fresh pasta cooks in about 2 minutes after the water returns to a boil, dried pasta in 5 to 10 minutes.*
• *Cook only until al dente (tender but firm).*
• *Drain cooked pasta in a colander or strainer and use immediately.*

ROTINI WITH SALMON AND CHIVES

Here's a quick and easy cream sauce that's perfect for pasta. You simply boil whipping cream. This rich dish goes well with a green salad and a light fresh fruit dessert. (photo, p. 131)

2 cups	rotini (about 1/4 lb/125 g)	500 mL
1-1/2 cups	whipping cream	375 mL
1	can (7-3/4 oz/ 220 g) sockeye salmon, drained	1
1/4 cup	(approx) freshly grated Parmesan cheese	50 mL
2 tbsp	chopped fresh chives or green onion	25 mL
	Salt and pepper	

• In large pot of boiling salted water, cook rotini according to package directions or until al dente (tender but firm); drain well.
• Meanwhile, in skillet, bring cream to boil; boil for 3 minutes or until reduced and slightly thickened. Stir in salmon, cheese and drained cooked pasta; toss lightly.
• Sprinkle with chives and season with salt and pepper to taste. Pass extra Parmesan separately, if desired. Makes 4 to 6 first-course or 2 or 3 main-course servings.

SPAGHETTI WITH SAUSAGE AND TOMATO SAUCE

Spicy Italian sausage adds lots of flavor to a quick tomato sauce.

2 tbsp	olive oil	25 mL
1/2 cup	diced onion	125 mL
1/2 cup	sliced mushrooms	125 mL
1	clove garlic, minced	1
1/2 lb	sweet or hot Italian sausages	250 g
1	can (19 oz/540 mL) tomatoes	1
1/4 tsp	each dried basil and oregano	1 mL
	Salt and pepper	
3/4 lb	spaghetti	375 g
	Freshly grated Parmesan cheese	

• In skillet, heat oil over medium heat; add onion, mushrooms and garlic and cook for about 5 minutes or until onion is softened and translucent. Transfer to small bowl and set aside.
• Remove casings from sausages. In same skillet, cook sausage meat over medium-high heat, stirring and breaking up large pieces, for about 6 minutes or until browned.
• Chop tomatoes coarsely and add to skillet along with their juice. Stir in reserved onion mixture, basil and oregano; cook over medium-high heat, stirring occasionally, for 5 minutes. Season with salt and pepper to taste.
• Meanwhile, in large pot of boiling salted water, cook spaghetti until al dente (tender but firm); drain. Serve with sauce spooned over and sprinkle with Parmesan to taste. Makes about 4 servings.

BROCCOLI PASTA

This light but satisfying main course is a welcome change from meat and potatoes.

1	**bunch fresh broccoli (about 1-1/2 lb/750 g)**	1
1	**pkg (375 g) fine egg noodles**	1
1/4 cup	**vegetable oil**	50 mL
1/4 cup	**butter**	50 mL
1	**small onion, finely chopped**	1
1	**large clove garlic, finely chopped**	1
2 tbsp	**dry vermouth or white wine**	25 mL
	Salt and pepper	
	Freshly grated Parmesan cheese	

• Cut broccoli into florets; peel and chop stems. In small amount of boiling salted water, cook broccoli for 3 to 4 minutes or until tender-crisp. Drain and set aside.

• In saucepan of boiling water, cook noodles according to package instructions or until al dente (tender but firm). Drain well and transfer to serving bowl.

• Meanwhile, in large skillet or heavy saucepan, heat oil with butter over medium heat; cook onion and garlic for 3 to 4 minutes or until tender. Stir in vermouth and bring to boil. Add broccoli and heat through.

• Add to noodles and toss thoroughly. Season with salt and pepper to taste. Sprinkle liberally with Parmesan and serve immediately; pass extra Parmesan. Makes 3 or 4 main-course servings.

Broccoli Pasta

GNOCCHI WITH FOUR CHEESES

Serve this richly sauced dish with Italian corn bread and a salad of tiny frozen peas, thawed but not cooked, tossed with watercress and chopped red onion in a herb dressing.

1/4 lb	Gorgonzola, Roquefort or Stilton cheese, crumbled	125 g
1/4 lb	Jarlsberg cheese, cubed	125 g
1/4 lb	Fontina cheese, cubed	125 g
1/4 lb	Havarti cheese, cubed	125 g
1 cup	light cream	250 mL
Pinch	each cayenne pepper and nutmeg	Pinch
	Pepper	
	Dry white wine (optional)	
3/4 lb	gnocchi	375 g
	Chopped fresh parsley	

- In large heavy saucepan or flameproof casserole, combine Gorgonzola, Jarlsberg, Fontina and Havarti cheeses; cook over low heat, stirring constantly, until completely melted. (Some butterfat will separate from cheese but mixture will become smooth as cheeses melt.)
- Gradually add cream, stirring constantly. Season with cayenne, nutmeg, and pepper to taste. Stir until smooth and heated through. (If sauce becomes stringy or starts to separate, stir in up to 2 tsp/10 mL white wine or chicken stock; cook over medium-low heat, stirring constantly, until smooth.)
- Meanwhile, in large pot of boiling salted water, cook gnocchi until al dente (tender but firm); drain. Add gnocchi to cheese mixture; stir to coat well. Garnish with parsley. Makes about 4 servings.

SPAGHETTI CARBONARA

Fast and delicious, this is also a good method for fettuccine or linguine.

1/2 lb	spaghetti	250 g
2 tbsp	butter	25 mL
1/2 cup	finely chopped bacon or pancetta	125 mL
1/4 cup	minced onion	50 mL
	Salt and pepper	
2	eggs, beaten	2
1/4 cup	milk	50 mL
1/4 cup	freshly grated Parmesan cheese	50 mL

- In saucepan of boiling salted water, cook spaghetti until al dente (tender but firm). Drain well.
- Meanwhile, in large heavy saucepan or skillet, melt butter; cook bacon until nearly crisp; add onion and cook until softened. Add hot drained spaghetti to pan; toss well. Season with salt and pepper to taste.
- Beat together eggs, milk and Parmesan; pour over spaghetti and toss well. Serve immediately; pass extra Parmesan and black pepper to grind coarsely on top. Makes 4 servings.

ASSORTED PASTAS

- **Agnolotti—small, filled, crescent-shaped semicircles**
- **Cannelloni—large, hollow rounds usually stuffed, then baked**
- **Gnocchi—little pasta dumplings, sometimes made with the addition of potatoes**
- **Lasagna—flat, broad noodles, usually baked in layers with cheese and sauces**
- **Mezzaluna—stuffed pasta shaped like half-moons**
- **Ravioli—stuffed pasta squares**
- **Tortellini—small, stuffed crescents**

SMALL PASTAS

- **Acini Pepe—little pasta buckshots**
- **Alfabeti—alphabet pasta**
- **Anellini—little rings**
- **Elbows—small, curved tubes**
- **Orzo—known as "pasta barley," shaped like rice**
- **Shells—small, shell-shaped pasta, available in many sizes**
- **Stelline—small, star-shaped pasta**
- **Squares—flat pasta cut into squares**

PENNE WITH SWEET PEPPERS AND TWO CHEESES

For a quick supper, serve this dish with crusty bread and a spinach salad sprinkled with bacon bits. Frozen yogurt makes a light ending to the meal. If penne is not available, substitute any other tubular pasta such as rigatoni or fusilli.

2 tbsp	olive oil	25 mL
1	onion, coarsely chopped	1
1	each sweet green and red pepper, cut in strips	1
1 tbsp	finely chopped fresh sage (or 1 tsp/5 mL dried)	15 mL
2	cloves garlic, minced	2
1 tbsp	all-purpose flour	15 mL
1-1/4 cups	light cream or milk	300 mL
1 lb	penne	500 g
1/2 lb	Swiss cheese, shredded	250 g
1 cup	freshly grated Parmesan cheese	250 mL
1/2 tsp	pepper	2 mL
1/4 tsp	hot pepper flakes	1 mL

• In large skillet, heat oil over medium-high heat; cook onion for about 2 minutes or until softened. Add green and red peppers, sage and garlic; cook for about 3 minutes or until peppers are softened.
• Stir in flour; cook, stirring constantly, for 1 minute. Stir in cream; cook, stirring constantly, for 2 to 3 minutes or until slightly thickened. Remove from heat and set aside.
• Meanwhile, in large pot of boiling water, cook pasta until al dente (tender but firm); drain.
• In large serving bowl, stir together Swiss and Parmesan cheeses, pepper and hot pepper flakes. Add pasta and sweet pepper mixture to bowl; toss gently. Serve immediately. Makes 4 generous servings.

TWO-PEPPER PASTA WITH PROSCIUTTO

Sturdy rigatoni is a good pasta to use for this colorful dish, which has just a hint of hot pepper. Serve with a slaw of red and green cabbage and celery in a creamy dressing.

1	sweet red pepper	1
1	sweet green pepper	1
1	large onion	1
2 tbsp	olive oil	25 mL
1 tbsp	butter	15 mL
1	clove garlic, minced	1
1/4 cup	chicken stock	50 mL
1/4 tsp	crushed green peppercorns	1 mL
Pinch	hot pepper flakes	Pinch
3/4 lb	rigatoni	375 g
2 cups	shredded mozzarella cheese	500 mL
1/4 lb	prosciutto, cut in thin strips	125 g
	Salt and pepper	

• Halve and seed red and green peppers; cut into 1/4-inch (5 mm) wide strips. Cut onion lengthwise into 1/4-inch (5 mm) wide strips.
• In large skillet, heat oil with butter over medium heat; add peppers, onion and garlic and cook for about 5 minutes or until onion is softened and translucent.
• Add stock, peppercorns and hot pepper flakes; increase heat to medium-high and cook for 2 to 3 minutes or until liquid is slightly thickened. Turn heat off but leave skillet on burner.
• Meanwhile, in large pot of boiling salted water, cook rigatoni until al dente (tender but firm); drain. Add rigatoni to skillet; toss to coat well. Add mozzarella and prosciutto; mix just until cheese has melted (over medium-low heat if necessary). Season with salt and pepper to taste. Makes about 4 servings.

SHORT PASTAS
• **Cavatelli**—little, hollow shells with a rough surface
• **Farfalle**—butterfly-shaped pasta, also called bow ties
• **Fusilli**—small twists of pasta
• **Penne**—short, narrow tubes cut like quills or pens
• **Radiatore**—short, stubby tubes with frills all around
• **Rigatoni**—large, penne-like pasta with grooves
• **Rotelle**—shaped like wheels
• **Rotini**—large twists of pasta
• **Ziti**—large, hollow tubes cut into 2-inch (5 cm) lengths

Fusilli with Tomato-Vegetable Primavera

FUSILLI WITH TOMATO-VEGETABLE PRIMAVERA

This colorful satisfying pasta dish makes a terrific family supper. Fruit and cheese for dessert will ensure adequate protein in the meal.

1/4 lb	yellow beans	125 g
1/4 lb	asparagus	125 g
Half	sweet red pepper	Half
Half	sweet green pepper	Half
2 tbsp	butter	25 mL
1	clove garlic, minced	1
1	carrot, thinly sliced diagonally	1
1/4 cup	chicken stock or water	50 mL
1	can (14 oz/ 398 mL) tomato sauce	1
1/2 cup	pitted black olives	125 mL
1 tsp	dried basil	5 mL
1/2 tsp	dried oregano	2 mL
3/4 lb	long or short fusilli	375 g
	Salt and pepper	
2	green onions, chopped	2
1/4 cup	freshly grated Parmesan cheese	50 mL

• Trim beans and asparagus; cut diagonally into 1-inch (2.5 cm) lengths. Seed and cut red and green peppers into strips.

• In large skillet, preferably nonstick, melt butter over medium-high heat; cook beans and garlic, stirring, for 2 minutes. Add asparagus, red and green peppers and carrot; cook for about 1 minute or until slightly softened.

• Pour in stock; cover and steam for 2 to 3 minutes or until vegetables are tender-crisp. Add tomato sauce, olives, basil and oregano; cook until heated through. Season with salt and pepper to taste.

• Meanwhile, in large pot of boiling salted water, cook pasta until al dente (tender but firm). Drain and toss with sauce. Sprinkle with green onions and Parmesan. Makes 4 servings.

LINGUINE AND FETTUCCINE WITH SPRING LEEKS AND ZUCCHINI

Linguine and Fettuccine with Spring Leeks and Zucchini

Fresh basil gives a delightful flavor, but if it isn't available, substitute 1/4 cup (50 mL) chopped fresh parsley and 1-1/2 tsp (7 mL) dried basil. Chop basil leaves just before using, otherwise they'll darken.

1/4 cup	chicken stock	50 mL
4 cups	julienne leeks (white parts only)	1 L
2-1/2 cups	julienne zucchini	625 mL
1/2 lb	linguine	250 g
1/2 lb	spinach or basil fettuccine	250 g
3	eggs, lightly beaten	3
1/2 cup	milk	125 mL
1/2 cup	thinly sliced radishes	125 mL
1/4 cup	chopped fresh basil	50 mL
1/4 cup	freshly grated Parmesan cheese	50 mL
	Pepper	

• In skillet, bring chicken stock to boil. Add leeks and zucchini; simmer for 2 minutes or until tender-crisp.

• In large pot of boiling salted water, cook linguine and fettuccine until al dente (tender but firm); drain and return to saucepan. Combine eggs with milk; add to drained noodles and mix well (heat of noodles will cook eggs). Add zucchini mixture, radishes, basil and Parmesan; toss well. Sprinkle each serving with pepper to taste. Makes 6 to 8 servings.

FETTUCCINE WITH MUSHROOM AND CLAM SAUCE

Mushrooms and clams make fashionably light toppings for pasta.

1/2 lb	fettuccine	250 g
1 tbsp	butter	15 mL
2 cups	sliced mushrooms	500 mL
1/4 cup	chopped green onions	50 mL
2	cloves garlic, minced	2
1/2 cup	whipping cream	125 mL
1/4 cup	dry white wine	50 mL
1	can (5 oz/142 g) clams, drained	1
2 tbsp	chopped fresh parsley	25 mL
	Freshly grated Parmesan cheese	

• In saucepan of boiling salted water, cook fettuccine until al dente (tender but firm). Drain well.

• Meanwhile, in skillet, heat butter; sauté mushrooms, onions and garlic until tender. Add cream and wine; simmer for 1 minute. Add clams and parsley; simmer for 2 minutes.

• Pour sauce over hot drained fettuccine; toss well. Sprinkle with Parmesan and serve immediately. Makes 4 servings.

TORTELLINI IN CREAM SAUCE

Fresh or frozen tortellini (meat- or cheese-stuffed) are available in many supermarkets now, and are great with any simple tomato sauce. This creamy cheese sauce makes a nice change and couldn't be easier to make.

1/2 lb	tortellini	250 g
1 cup	whipping cream	250 mL
1 cup	shredded mozzarella cheese	250 mL
1 cup	freshly grated Parmesan cheese	250 mL
	Salt and pepper	

• In pot of boiling salted water, cook tortellini until tender; drain.

• Meanwhile, in large saucepan or skillet, bring cream to gentle boil; simmer for about 2 minutes until slightly thickened. Remove from heat and gradually add cheeses, stirring until melted.

• Add drained tortellini to sauce; season lightly with salt and generously with pepper. Serve immediately with more Parmesan to grate on top if desired. Makes about 4 servings.

QUICK MACARONI AND CHEESE

Here's a fast way to make macaroni and cheese from scratch. You can use any type of pasta. The sauce will thicken upon standing. Serve with a green salad or marinated vegetable salad and crusty bread.

1/2 lb	macaroni or noodles	250 g
2	eggs, lightly beaten	2
1/2 cup	milk	125 mL
1 tbsp	butter	15 mL
2 cups	shredded Cheddar cheese (about 8 oz/ 250 g)	500 mL
	Salt and pepper	

• In large pot of boiling salted water, cook noodles according to package directions or until al dente (tender but firm); drain well and return to pot.

• Add eggs, milk and butter; toss to mix. Stir in cheese and cook over low heat, stirring constantly, for 1 to 2 minutes or until cheese has melted and sauce has thickened slightly. Season with salt and pepper to taste. Makes 4 servings.

LONG, THIN PASTAS

• **Bucatini—hollow, spaghetti-like strands**
• **Capellini—very thin strands, often called angel-hair pasta**
• **Fettuccine—pasta ribbons about 1/4 inch (5 mm) wide**
• **Linguine—narrow, flat spaghetti**
• **Spaghetti—the most familiar pasta strands**
• **Spaghettini—thin spaghetti**
• **Vermicelli—thin strands, thicker than capellini and thinner than spaghettini**

PARSLEY-LEMON ORZO

The tiny rice-shaped pasta called orzo makes an interesting replacement for rice as a side dish.

8 cups	light chicken stock	2 L
2 cups	orzo	500 mL
1 tbsp	butter	15 mL
1/2 cup	minced fresh parsley	125 mL
	Grated rind of 1 lemon	
	Salt and pepper	

• In large saucepan, bring stock to boil. Add orzo and cook, uncovered, for about 7 minutes or just until tender; drain thoroughly. (Stock may be reused for soup.)
• Toss orzo with butter, parsley, lemon rind, lots of pepper to taste and a little salt, if needed. Serve immediately. Makes about 6 servings.

VARIATION:

PARSLEY-LEMON RICE:
• Rice may be substituted for orzo; cook 1-1/2 cups (375 mL) rice in 3 cups (750 mL) chicken stock (use 3-3/4 cups/925 mL stock if using parboiled rice).

SPEEDY LENTIL AND BEAN CASSEROLE

While lentils are not technically grains (they are called legumes or pulses), they are high in fibre and low in fat. This casserole is quick to prepare.

1 tbsp	vegetable oil	15 mL
2	stalks celery, sliced	2
1	large onion, chopped	1
1	can (19 oz/ 540 mL) kidney beans, drained	1
1	can (19 oz/ 540 mL) lentils, drained	1
1	can (19 oz/ 540 mL) tomatoes, drained and chopped	1
1/2 tsp	dried rosemary or thyme	2 mL
	Pepper	
1-1/2 cups	shredded Cheddar cheese	375 mL

• In flameproof casserole, heat oil over medium heat; cook celery and onion for 4 minutes or until onion is softened.
• Add beans, lentils, tomatoes, rosemary, and pepper to taste; bring to simmer, stirring occasionally. Sprinkle with cheese; broil until cheese melts. Makes about 4 servings.

Pasta with Artichokes and Pine Nuts

PASTA WITH ARTICHOKES AND PINE NUTS

Take advantage of fast stove-top cooking methods, especially stir-frying, when you don't have time to spare. Serve this pasta with bread sticks and black olives. A mild cheese and fresh apple or pear wedges round out the meal.

2 cups	small pasta shells or elbow macaroni	500 mL
1	jar (6 oz/170 mL) marinated artichokes	1
1	small onion, chopped	1
1	small sweet red pepper, slivered	1
2 tbsp	pine nuts	25 mL
1	clove garlic, minced	1
1/3 cup	freshly grated Parmesan cheese	75 mL
1/3 cup	sour cream	75 mL
	Salt and pepper	

• In large pot of boiling salted water, cook pasta according to package directions or until al dente (tender but firm); drain and set aside.

• Meanwhile, drain artichokes, reserving marinade in wok or heavy skillet; cut artichokes into quarters and set aside.

• Heat marinade in wok over medium-high heat until hot but not smoking. Add onion, red pepper, nuts and garlic. Stir-fry for about 5 minutes or until nuts are golden and vegetables are tender-crisp; do not let garlic or nuts get too brown. Add drained artichokes; cook until heated through, 1 to 2 minutes.

• Remove from heat; add pasta, Parmesan and sour cream. Toss together; season with salt and pepper to taste. Serve immediately. Makes 4 servings.

PASTA WITH CHICK-PEAS

This quick, tasty and hearty dish is a great budget supper. Substitute other small pasta shapes, such as elbow macaroni, if tubetti is unavailable.

2 tbsp	vegetable oil	25 mL
1	onion, finely chopped	1
1	clove garlic, minced	1
1	can (19 oz/540 mL) tomatoes (undrained), chopped	1
1/2 tsp	dried basil	2 mL
	Salt and pepper	
1	can (14 oz/398 mL) chick-peas, drained	1
3/4 lb	tubetti	375 g
1/2 cup	freshly grated Parmesan cheese	125 mL
2 tbsp	chopped fresh parsley	25 mL

• In saucepan, heat oil over medium heat; cook onion and garlic, uncovered, until softened, about 4 minutes.
• Add tomatoes, basil, and salt and pepper to taste; simmer, uncovered, over medium heat for about 20 minutes or until thickened. Add chick-peas; cook for about 5 minutes or until heated through.
• Meanwhile, in large pot of boiling salted water, cook pasta until al dente (tender but firm); drain well. Toss pasta with tomato sauce. Sprinkle with Parmesan and parsley. Makes 4 to 6 servings.

Pasta with Chick-Peas

RICE WITH BROCCOLI AND TOMATOES

This makes a colorful accompaniment to simple chicken and chops.

2-1/2 cups	chicken stock	625 mL
1 cup	long-grain rice	250 mL
1 tbsp	butter	15 mL
1 tsp	salt	5 mL
1	small onion, chopped	1
1	small bunch broccoli (about 1/2 lb/250 g), coarsely chopped	1
3	tomatoes, chopped, or 1 can (19 oz/540 mL), drained and chopped	3
	Pepper	

• In saucepan, bring stock to boil; stir in rice, butter, salt, onion and broccoli. Reduce heat to medium; cover and cook until stock is absorbed, about 20 minutes. Stir in tomatoes, and pepper to taste. Makes 4 generous servings.

COUSCOUS

Couscous is finely cracked durum wheat or coarse semolina that has been steamed and dried. It is used as a pasta-type food in North African and Moroccan menus. Precooked couscous is available at Middle Eastern and natural food stores and some supermarkets.

• In saucepan, bring 1-3/4 cups (425 mL) chicken stock or water to boil. Stir in 1 cup (250 mL) precooked couscous. Cover and let stand for 5 minutes. Fluff with fork. Makes 4 cups (1 L).

Optional Additions:
• Sauté 1 small onion, chopped and 1/2 cup (125 mL) sliced mushrooms in 1 tbsp (15 mL) butter. Toss with reconstituted couscous.
• Add 1 tbsp (15 mL) chopped fresh basil and 2 slivered sun-dried tomatoes to reconstituted couscous.
• Add 1/3 cup (75 mL) plumped raisins, currants, chopped dried apricots or chopped pitted prunes.
• Fluff couscous, adding 1/3 cup (75 mL) chopped toasted walnuts or pecans, or toasted slivered or sliced almonds.
• Add 1/2 cup (125 mL) frozen peas and 1 tbsp (15 mL) chopped fresh mint to chicken stock, along with couscous.

RICE PILAF

Rice should take 20 to 25 minutes to cook to perfection. If it takes longer for the rice to absorb the liquid, the heat is too low and the rice will be overcooked; if it takes only 10 minutes, the heat is too high and the rice will still be hard.

3 tbsp	butter	50 mL
1	onion, finely chopped	1
1	sweet green pepper, diced	1
1	tomato, peeled, seeded and chopped	1
1-1/2 cups	long-grain rice	375 mL
3 cups	chicken stock	750 mL
	Salt and pepper	
2 tbsp	butter	25 mL
3 tbsp	chopped fresh parsley	50 mL

• In 12-cup (3 L) saucepan, melt butter and cook onion until tender. Add green pepper and tomato; cook until any liquid has evaporated and pepper has softened slightly. Add rice and stir to mix well.
• Pour in stock and bring to boil; reduce heat, cover and simmer gently for 20 to 25 minutes or until liquid is absorbed. Season with salt and pepper to taste. Stir in butter, then parsley. Makes 6 servings.

ORANGE RICE AND RED LENTIL PILAF

Here's an alternative to plain rice side dishes. Red lentils add interest and nutritional value to this pilaf.

2 tbsp	butter	25 mL
1	onion, chopped	1
1	clove garlic, minced	1
1/2 cup	parboiled rice	125 mL
1/2 tsp	curry powder	2 mL
3/4 cup	chicken stock	175 mL
3/4 cup	unsweetened orange juice	175 mL
1/2 cup	split red lentils, rinsed and sorted	125 mL
1/4 cup	raisins	50 mL
1/2 tsp	grated orange rind	2 mL

• In saucepan, heat butter over medium-high heat; cook onion and garlic until softened, about 3 minutes. Stir in rice and curry powder; cook, stirring, for 1 minute.
• Add chicken stock and orange juice; bring to boil. Reduce heat to low and cook, covered, for 10 minutes.
• Stir in lentils; cover and cook for 10 to 15 minutes, stirring halfway through, or until lentils and rice are tender and liquid has been absorbed. Let stand, covered, for 5 minutes. Stir in raisins and orange rind. Makes 4 to 6 servings.

Vegetables

Here are vegetable dishes you do have time to cook. And with handy kitchen tools like food processors, woks and microwave ovens, you can make short work of vegetable preparation. Even without these extras, fresh and fast rush-hour meals can still include good-for-you vegetables. With recipes such as Orange-Glazed Beets and Green Beans with Garlic and Sesame Seeds, even kids will like veggies. In this section we also offer dishes like Jiffy Bean Casserole, Ratatouille and Chick-Peas, and California Stuffed Zucchini, which you can serve as main courses in marvelous meatless meals.

SAVORY VEGETABLE RING

This colorful vegetable wreath will brighten any dinner menu. It makes a particularly delightful contrast to fish.

1	small tomato, cut in wedges	1
2 cups	broccoli florets	500 mL
2 cups	cauliflower florets	500 mL
1/4 cup	butter	50 mL
1	small clove garlic, minced	1
1/2 tsp	dried basil	2 mL
1/4 tsp	dry mustard	1 mL

- Place tomato wedges in 4-cup (1 L) ovenproof ring mould; set aside.
- In large saucepan, steam broccoli and cauliflower for about 5 minutes or until tender-crisp; drain. Snugly pack into ring mould over tomato wedges.
- In small saucepan, melt butter; stir in garlic, basil and mustard. Pour over vegetables; cover with foil. Bake in 350°F (180°C) oven for 10 minutes or until heated through. Invert onto serving platter and unmould. Makes 4 servings.

GREEN BEAN AND CELERY SAUTÉ

Celery adds extra flavor and crunch to this vegetable dish, which goes well with any kind of meat.

1-1/2 lb	green beans, trimmed	750 g
1/4 cup	butter	50 mL
1	onion, minced	1
2	cloves garlic, minced	2
2 cups	sliced celery	500 mL
	Salt and pepper	

- In large pot of boiling water, cook beans for 3 to 4 minutes or until tender-crisp. Drain and set aside.
- Meanwhile, in large skillet, melt butter; cook onion and garlic over medium heat for 3 to 4 minutes or until softened. Add celery and cook, stirring often, until tender-crisp, 3 to 4 minutes. Stir in green beans and cook until heated through. Season with salt and pepper to taste. Makes about 6 servings.

Savory Vegetable Ring

GREEN BEANS WITH GARLIC AND SESAME SEEDS

Green beans are enhanced with garlic and crunchy sesame seeds in this easy flavorful dish. Substitute chopped red pepper or slivered almonds to taste for the sesame seeds if you like. The recipe can be easily halved.

2 lb	green beans (fresh or frozen)	1 kg
2 tbsp	sesame seeds	25 mL
1/4 cup	butter	50 mL
4	cloves garlic, minced	4
	Salt and pepper	

- Trim green beans, if using fresh. In pot of boiling water, cook beans until tender-crisp, about 5 minutes for fresh or 1 minute for frozen. Drain.
- In skillet, toast sesame seeds over medium-high heat for 2 minutes, shaking pan constantly.
- In saucepan, melt butter over medium heat; cook garlic, stirring, for 30 seconds. Add hot beans, sesame seeds, and salt and pepper to taste; toss to mix. Makes about 8 servings.

JIFFY BEAN CASSEROLE

Kidney and romano beans, tomato and spinach make a colorful tasty combination.

1 tbsp	vegetable oil	15 mL
1	clove garlic, minced	1
2	onions, sliced	2
1	can (14 oz/398 mL) tomatoes	1
1	can (19 oz/540 mL) red kidney beans, drained	1
1	can (19 oz/540 mL) romano beans, drained	1
1	can (12 oz/341 mL) corn kernels	1
1 tsp	dried oregano	5 mL
1	pkg (10 oz/284 g) fresh spinach, coarsely chopped	1
	Salt and pepper	

- In heavy saucepan or casserole, heat oil over medium heat; cook garlic and onions, stirring occasionally, for 3 minutes or until tender.
- Add tomatoes, breaking up large pieces. Add kidney and romano beans, corn and oregano; bring to simmer. Add spinach; cover and simmer for about 2 minutes or until wilted. Season with salt and pepper to taste. Makes 4 servings.

VEGETABLE SAUTÉ

Here's an easy but interesting and delicious way to serve vegetables. Use any colorful combination you have on hand. Add longest-cooking vegetables to pan first, the shortest-cooking ones last. (photo, p. 10)

2 tbsp	vegetable oil	25 mL
2	carrots, diagonally sliced	2
2	stalks celery, diagonally sliced	2
1	sweet red and/or green pepper and/or small zucchini, diagonally sliced	1
1	large clove garlic, minced	1
1/4 cup	chicken stock	50 mL
1/4 lb	snow peas (or half 10 oz/284 g pkg, frozen, thawed)	125 g
	Salt and pepper	

- In wok or skillet, heat oil over medium-high heat; stir-fry carrots for 1 minute. Add celery; stir-fry for 1 minute. Add red pepper and garlic; stir-fry for 1 minute.
- Add chicken stock; cover and steam for 1 minute. Add snow peas; cover and cook for 1 minute or until tender-crisp. Season with salt and pepper to taste. Makes 4 servings.

Ratatouille and Chick-Peas

RATATOUILLE AND CHICK-PEAS

For a great meatless meal, serve this colorful dish with nutty multigrain bread and a green salad. Finish with fresh fruit and cheese.

2	red onions, chopped	2
2	zucchini, sliced	2
1	eggplant, peeled and cubed (about 2 lb/1 kg total)	1
1	can (19 oz/ 540 mL) plum tomatoes (undrained)	1
2	cloves garlic, minced	2
2 tsp	dried oregano	10 mL
1	can (19 oz/540 mL) chick-peas, drained	1
	Salt and pepper	

• In skillet or large saucepan, combine onions, zucchini, eggplant, tomatoes, garlic and oregano; bring to boil, stirring and breaking up tomatoes with wooden spoon. Reduce heat and simmer, covered, for 20 minutes.

• Rinse chick-peas under cold running water and stir into skillet; simmer, uncovered, for about 10 minutes or until excess moisture has evaporated and sauce has thickened slightly. Season with salt and pepper to taste. Makes 4 servings.

• **Microwave Directions:** In 8-cup (2 L) microwaveable casserole, combine onions, zucchini and eggplant. Microwave, covered, at High for 3 minutes. Drain off any liquid.

• Thoroughly drain tomatoes, reserving juice for another use. Stir tomatoes into vegetable mixture, breaking them up. Add garlic, oregano and rinsed well-drained chick-peas; mix well. Microwave at High for 4 minutes or until vegetables are tender. Let stand, covered, for 5 minutes. Season with salt and pepper to taste.

CALIFORNIA STUFFED ZUCCHINI

Crunchy nuts and chewy dried fruit give character to this colorful dish. Add a dark bread and a pot of whipped butter for a light lunch.

4	medium zucchini	4
2 tbsp	butter	25 mL
2 tbsp	finely chopped onion	25 mL
2	carrots, coarsely grated	2
1/4 cup	chopped walnuts	50 mL
1/4 cup	whole wheat bread crumbs	50 mL
2 tbsp	raisins, finely chopped	25 mL
1/2 cup	shredded Monterey Jack cheese	125 mL

• Cut zucchini in half lengthwise. With spoon, scoop out pulp leaving 1/2-inch (1 cm) thick shells. Coarsely chop pulp and reserve.

• In saucepan of lightly salted boiling water, cook zucchini halves for 3 minutes or until tender but still firm; drain well. Place cut sides up in lightly greased baking dish.

• In skillet, melt butter over medium-high heat; sauté onion for 2 minutes or until softened. Add carrots along with reserved chopped zucchini; stir-fry for 3 minutes or until softened. Add walnuts, bread crumbs, raisins and half of the cheese; stir well.

• Spoon into zucchini halves mounding mixture in shells; sprinkle with remaining cheese. Bake in 350°F (180°C) oven for 8 to 10 minutes or until heated through and cheese melts. Makes 4 servings.

California Stuffed Zucchini

SAUTÉED CHERRY TOMATOES WITH FRESH BASIL

Take care not to overcook this flavorful side dish.

2 tbsp	olive oil	25 mL
2 cups	cherry tomatoes	500 mL
2	cloves garlic, minced	2
2	green onions, finely chopped	2
1/4 cup	chopped fresh basil	50 mL
	Salt and pepper	

• In large skillet, heat oil over medium-high heat; cook tomatoes, garlic and onions, shaking pan occasionally, for about 3 minutes or until tomatoes are tender.
• Remove to serving dish and sprinkle with basil; season with salt and pepper to taste. Makes 4 servings.

VARIATION:

SAUTÉED SNOW PEAS AND CHERRY TOMATOES:
• Toss 1-1/2 cups (375 mL) snow peas with the oil, garlic and green onions for a minute before adding the cherry tomatoes. Continue cooking, shaking pan occasionally, until tomatoes are tender and snow peas are bright green and tender-crisp. Makes 4 to 6 servings. (photo, p. 15)

ORANGE-GLAZED BEETS

Here's a vegetable side dish that is fast and easy to prepare.

2	cans (each 14 oz/ 398 mL) beets	2
2 tbsp	butter	25 mL
1 tbsp	frozen orange juice concentrate	15 mL
1 tbsp	liquid honey	15 mL
	Salt and pepper	
1 tsp	grated orange rind	5 mL

• Drain beets thoroughly and slice.
• In skillet, heat butter over medium heat; stir in orange juice concentrate, honey and beets. Cook, stirring, for 3 to 5 minutes or until heated through. Season with salt and pepper to taste. Sprinkle with orange rind. Makes about 4 to 6 servings.

ASPARAGUS AND BUTTON MUSHROOM STIR-FRY

For a speedy stir-fry, use the smallest mushrooms available. Serve this with grilled, steamed or poached fish or simple chicken dishes.

1 lb	asparagus or broccoli	500 g
3/4 lb	mushrooms (preferably button)	375 g
1/4 cup	butter	50 mL
1/2 tsp	salt	2 mL
Pinch	pepper	Pinch

• Trim bottoms of asparagus stalks and mushrooms. Slice asparagus diagonally into 1/2-inch (1 cm) wide slices. Cut mushrooms, if necessary, into 1-inch (2.5 cm) pieces.
• In wok or large skillet, melt butter over medium-high heat; add asparagus and stir to coat. Cover and cook for 2 minutes, shaking wok 2 or 3 times.
• Increase heat to high and add mushrooms, salt and pepper; stir well. Cover and cook for 1 minute. Uncover and stir-fry for 2 to 3 minutes longer or until asparagus is tender-crisp, mushrooms are softened and moisture has evaporated. Serve immediately. Makes 4 servings.

POTATO-ZUCCHINI PANCAKES

Potato-Zucchini
Pancakes

Serve these crisp, pan-fried patties with egg dishes, meat dishes or on their own with a dollop of sour cream or applesauce. The quickest way to grate the potatoes and zucchini is in a food processor.

2	potatoes (unpeeled)	2
1	zucchini (6 in/ 15 cm), unpeeled	1
1/3 cup	all-purpose flour	75 mL
1	egg, lightly beaten	1
	Salt and pepper	
2 tbsp	(approx) butter	25 mL
2 tbsp	(approx) vegetable oil	25 mL
2	small cloves garlic, cut in half	2

• Grate potatoes and zucchini; place on tea towel and rub gently to dry.
• In large bowl, mix together potatoes, zucchini and flour until vegetables are coated. Stir in egg; season with salt and pepper to taste.
• In large skillet, heat butter and oil over medium heat; cook garlic until golden, then discard.
• Using about 1/4 cup (50 mL) batter for each pancake, drop batter into hot fat; fry for 5 to 7 minutes or until golden on both sides, adding more butter and oil if necessary. Transfer to warm serving platter. Makes 8 pancakes.

JARLSBERG AND GREEN BEANS IN MUSTARD VINAIGRETTE

This tangy bean and cheese dish makes a delicious appetizer for summer barbecues or a light lunch on a hot day. Serve with country-style Italian bread.

1 lb	green beans	500 g
1/2 lb	Jarlsberg cheese	250 g
DRESSING:		
1	egg yolk	1
2 tbsp	grainy mustard	25 mL
1 tbsp	lemon juice	15 mL
2 tsp	minced fresh tarragon (or 1 tsp/5 mL dried)	10 mL
1/2 tsp	each salt and pepper	2 mL
Pinch	granulated sugar	Pinch
1	clove garlic, minced	1
1/3 cup	vegetable oil	75 mL

• Trim beans; cut into 2-inch (5 cm) lengths. In large saucepan of boiling salted water, cook beans until tender-crisp, 5 to 8 minutes. Drain and refresh under cold running water; pat dry. Transfer to large bowl. Cut cheese into strips same size as beans; add to beans.

• **Dressing:** Combine egg yolk, mustard, lemon juice, tarragon, salt, pepper, sugar and garlic; whisk in oil. Pour over bean mixture and toss. Taste and adjust seasoning if necessary. Serve immediately or refrigerate for up to 5 hours. Makes 4 to 6 appetizer-sized servings, 3 or 4 lunch servings.

Here are some quick additions to canned or frozen vegetables.
• **Herbs:** peas with parsley, dill or mint; carrots with rosemary or dill; brussels sprouts with chives.
• **Spices:** lima beans with mustard or paprika; carrots with cumin.
• **Nuts:** broccoli with almonds; carrots with walnuts or pecans.
• **Citrus:** asparagus with lemon and butter; brussels sprouts with lemon juice or white wine vinegar.
• **Bacon:** corn kernels or green beans topped with bacon bits.
• **Squash rings** with maple syrup.
• **Carrots** with honey.
• **Add-a-veg:** peas with sautéed green onions, celery or mushrooms; corn with sweet green or red pepper; broccoli with sliced onions and water chestnuts.

FRIED TOMATOES

These flavorful tomatoes are great as a side dish and terrific in pita sandwiches or warm salads. Be sure to use ripe but still firm tomatoes.

3	tomatoes	3
1/3 cup	olive oil	75 mL
4	cloves garlic, minced	4
1 tbsp	chopped fresh thyme (or 1/2 tsp/ 2 mL dried)	15 mL
1/4 tsp	hot pepper flakes	1 mL
2 tbsp	chopped fresh parsley	25 mL
	Salt	

• Core tomatoes. Cut into 1/2-inch (1 cm) thick slices. Pat dry with paper towels.
• In large skillet, heat oil over low heat; cook garlic, thyme and hot pepper flakes gently for about 2 minutes or until fragrant. Add tomatoes and cook, one layer at a time, for 3 to 5 minutes per side or until just beginning to soften. Using slotted spoon, transfer to serving dish. Sprinkle with parsley, and salt to taste. Makes about 6 servings.

JULIENNE OF CARROTS IN HONEY GLAZE

Carrots make a colorful accompaniment to any broiled or baked meat. This recipe cooks very quickly because the carrots are shredded into long strands.

1 lb	carrots	500 g
2 tbsp	unsalted butter	25 mL
1-1/2 tsp	liquid honey	7 mL
1 tsp	lemon juice	5 mL
	Pepper and nutmeg	

• Using vegetable peeler or food processor, shred carrots into long strands.
• In pot of boiling salted water, cook carrots for 1 to 2 minutes or until barely tender. Drain and refresh under cold running water; drain again.
• In skillet, melt butter over medium heat; stir in honey and lemon juice. Mix well. Add carrots; stir and toss for 2 to 3 minutes or until carrots are heated through and well coated. Season with pepper and nutmeg to taste. Makes 4 servings.

Desserts

Even on hectic days meals can have a sweet ending. Rely on simple bases such as ice creams, fruits and pound cakes to make easy desserts like Applesauce Angel Pudding or Dessert French Toast. Try our quick yet classy recipe for Souffléed Dessert Omelette or fill pretty glasses with Peach and Ricotta Parfait. Fruit and cheese combinations work well served in simple style or warmed up like Sautéed Pears and Brie. And check our chart (p. 155) for fast and easy dessert dress-ups.

APPLESAUCE ANGEL PUDDING

For everyday fare, make this pudding in a simple bowl. Dress it up for company by using a glass bowl so the layers show.

1	small angel cake (about 7 in/ 18 cm diameter)	1
1 cup	whipping cream	250 mL
2 tbsp	icing sugar	25 mL
1/2 tsp	cinnamon	2 mL
1	can (14 oz/398 mL) applesauce	1
2 tbsp	chopped nuts	25 mL

• Break angel cake into chunks. In mixing bowl, whip cream and icing sugar until stiff peaks form. Blend cinnamon into applesauce.
• In deep 6-cup (1.5 L) serving bowl, arrange alternating layers of half of the cake, half of the whipping cream and half of the applesauce; repeat layers. Sprinkle with nuts. Refrigerate until serving time. Makes 6 to 8 servings.

DESSERT FRENCH TOAST

This tasty treat with its dusting of icing sugar satisfies any sweet tooth when served with maple syrup.

3	eggs	3
1/3 cup	milk	75 mL
1/2 tsp	vanilla	2 mL
1 tbsp	(approx) butter	15 mL
6	slices pound cake, 1/2 inch (1 cm) thick	6
	Icing sugar	
1 tsp	grated lemon rind	5 mL
	Maple syrup (optional)	

• In mixing bowl, beat eggs, milk and vanilla until frothy.
• In skillet, melt butter over medium-high heat. Dip cake slices into egg mixture; add to skillet and cook, turning once and adding more butter if necessary, until golden brown.
• Remove from skillet and dust lightly with icing sugar. Sprinkle with lemon rind and serve immediately; pass maple syrup to pour over (if using). Makes 6 servings.

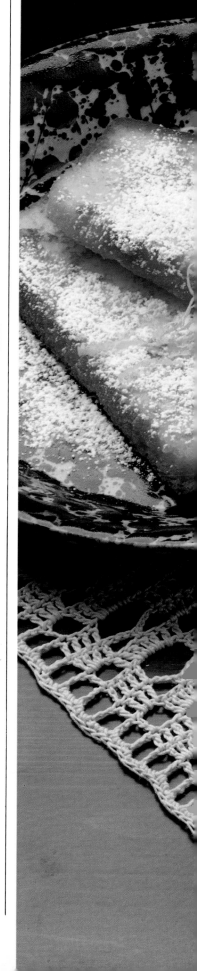

(Clockwise from top right) Applesauce Angel Pudding; Orange-Drizzled Cake Slices (p. 155); Dessert French Toast

SAUTÉED PEARS AND BRIE

The melted Brie resembles a sweet cheese fondue; however, you can substitute Camembert for Brie, and apples for pears for a completely different variation.

1 tbsp	butter	15 mL
3	firm ripe pears (Anjou or Bartlett), peeled and sliced	3
1 tbsp	packed brown sugar	15 mL
1 tbsp	brandy or lemon juice	15 mL
1/2 lb	Brie, cut in 4 pieces	250 g
1/4 cup	toasted chopped walnuts* (optional)	50 mL

• In heavy skillet, melt butter over medium-high heat; cook pears, stirring, for 3 to 5 minutes or until tender. Add sugar and brandy; stir until heated through. Add cheese and cook for 30 seconds or until cheese just starts to melt.
• Transfer to serving dish. Sprinkle with walnuts (if using). Makes 4 servings.
*To toast walnuts, spread on baking sheet and bake in 350°F (180°C) oven for 5 minutes or until golden.

Here's a quick rush-hour dessert: Make a rum and sour cream sauce by adding brown sugar and rum to taste to sour cream, then mixing with fresh grapes.

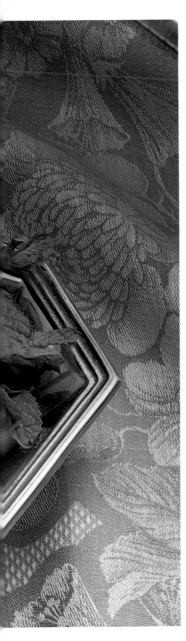

Sautéed Pears and Brie

ORANGE-DRIZZLED CAKE SLICES

On a chilly wintry evening, a warm citrus-flavored sauce on cake is often nicer than frosting. If you don't have cake, pour the sauce over thinly sliced bananas or ice cream. (photo, p. 153)

6	slices angel cake or pound cake	6
ORANGE SAUCE:		
1/4 cup	granulated sugar	50 mL
1 tbsp	cornstarch	15 mL
1 cup	orange juice	250 mL
1 tbsp	butter	15 mL
2 tsp	lemon juice	10 mL
1 tsp	grated orange rind	5 mL
	Shredded coconut (optional)	

• **Orange Sauce:** In small saucepan, mix together sugar and cornstarch; blend in orange juice. Cook over medium heat until mixture thickens and comes to boil. Remove from heat; stir in butter, lemon juice and orange rind. Let cool slightly.

• Arrange cake slices on baking sheet and broil until lightly toasted, if desired. Transfer to serving dishes and pour orange sauce evenly over tops. Sprinkle with coconut (if using). Makes 6 servings.

• **Microwave Directions:** In 4-cup (1 L) measure, combine sugar, cornstarch and orange juice. Microwave, covered, at High for 3 to 4 minutes or until mixture boils, stirring once. Blend in butter, lemon juice and orange rind. Proceed as above.

FAST FRUIT DESSERTS

Nothing could be simpler and more appealing for dessert than an attractive and interesting presentation of fruit.

Apple and pear slices served with cheese—your favorite variety.

Cantaloupe and honeydew melon slices sprinkled with orange juice and shredded coconut.

Fig halves served with whipped cream flavored with port.

Honeydew Melon balls or chunks drizzled with tequila, lime juice and grated lime rind.

Mango or papaya slices drizzled with lemon or lime juice.

Orange segments or slices sprinkled with orange liqueur.

Peach halves filled with mascarpone cheese flavored with amaretto, sprinkled with chopped toasted almonds.

Peach slices and blueberries with yogurt flavored with honey and cinnamon.

Peach slices topped with sweetened yogurt with an added pinch of cardamom and a sprinkle of toasted nuts.

Pear slices brushed with lemon juice and served with cambozola and toasted walnuts.

Pineapple wedges or slices topped with sliced strawberries and a dollop of brandy-flavored whipped cream.

Strawberries, whole, served with bowls of crème fraîche and Demerara-type sugar for dipping.

Other fast and easy fruit desserts:
Barbecued Banana Boats: Grill unpeeled bananas until soft to the touch, slice lengthwise but not through, and sprinkle with orange juice or liqueur.

Broiled Banana Slices: Sprinkle banana slices with rum or lemon juice and brown sugar and broil until sugar is bubbly.

Caramelized Oranges: Sprinkle orange segments or slices with brown sugar and broil.

Cinnamon Orange Compote: Sprinkle orange slices with sugar and cinnamon; drizzle with red wine.

Fast Fruit Brulée: Top strawberries and blueberries with whipped cream and a sprinkle of brown sugar. Broil until sugar has caramelized and is golden brown.

Grilled Pineapple Kabobs: Skewer and grill chunks of pineapple brushed with honey.

Sautéed Apple Slices: Sauté apple slices with butter; drizzle with maple syrup (or sprinkle with brown sugar) and brandy. Cook until warmed through.

Sour Cream Fruit Dip: Flavor sour cream with finely chopped preserved ginger and honey; serve with assorted fresh fruit.

Strawberries Romanoff: Sprinkle sliced strawberries with sugar and orange liqueur; fold into whipped cream.

Warm Citrus Sections: Sprinkle orange and grapefruit sections with brown sugar and dot with butter; broil until golden. Sprinkle with toasted coconut and almonds, or granola.

Yogurt Sundae: Layer frozen yogurt, granola and sliced fresh fruit in parfait glasses.

FROSTED ANGEL CAKE

When your rush-hour dinner requires a special dessert, this easy frosted cake will fill the bill. Frost the cake before you start the dinner, then let it mellow in the refrigerator as long as possible.

1	small angel cake (about 7 in/18 cm diameter)	1
3 tbsp	orange juice or sherry	50 mL
1 cup	whipping cream	250 mL
1/4 cup	icing sugar	50 mL
2 tbsp	unsweetened cocoa powder	25 mL
GARNISH (optional):		
	Toasted sliced almonds	
	Fresh orange slices	

• With skewer, poke holes in cake. Sprinkle cake with orange juice; set aside.
• Pour cream into mixing bowl. Sift together sugar and cocoa; blend into cream. Beat until spreading consistency but not buttery. Spread over top and sides of cake. Refrigerate until serving time. Garnish with almonds and orange slices (if using). Makes 8 servings.

STOVE-TOP RICE PUDDING

This hearty dessert can be served warm, at room temperature or chilled. For an interesting variation, prepare the night before and serve chilled, mixed with drained canned peaches or fruit cocktail.

2-1/2 cups	water	625 mL
1/2 cup	seedless raisins	125 mL
Pinch	salt	Pinch
1	stick (2 in/5 cm) cinnamon	1
1	strip lemon rind	1
1 cup	long-grain rice	250 mL
1-1/2 cups	light cream	375 mL
1/2 cup	granulated sugar	125 mL
2	egg yolks, beaten	2
1/2 tsp	vanilla	2 mL
1/2 tsp	ground cinnamon (optional)	2 mL

• In large saucepan, bring water, raisins, salt, cinnamon stick and lemon rind to boil; stir in rice. Reduce heat to low; cover and simmer until rice is tender and liquid is almost all absorbed, about 20 minutes.
• Combine cream and sugar; stir into rice mixture. Cook gently over low heat until mixture is creamy.
• Whisk a little hot rice mixture into egg yolks, then stir yolk mixture back into pan. Cook over medium-low heat until mixture thickens, about 1 minute. Remove from heat and stir in vanilla.
• Just before serving, remove cinnamon stick and lemon rind. Sprinkle with ground cinnamon (if using). Makes 4 generous servings.

ICE CREAM DRESS-UPS

• **Ice cream makes a fast and easy spur-of-the-moment dessert. For casual entertaining, serve it in stemmed glasses or on dessert plates.**
• **Make a quick sauce to pour over the ice cream by puréeing a package of frozen sweetened raspberries or strawberries.**
• **For a simple treat with tropical flavor, purée peeled, fresh peaches and serve over coconut ice cream.**

Dress up fresh or canned fruits with grated citrus rind, chopped nuts, shredded coconut, coarsely grated chocolate or a dollop of whipped cream. Or make fruit kabobs by threading apple and pineapple chunks onto skewers with mandarin orange segments, grapes and thick slices of banana. Serve as is with sour cream or yogurt for dipping or sprinkle the kabobs with ginger, baste with honey and broil or grill.

Peach and Ricotta Parfait

PEACH AND RICOTTA PARFAIT

You can use almost any other fruit, such as fresh berrries or canned pears or apricots, instead of peaches for this dessert.

1 lb	**ricotta or cottage cheese**	500 g
1	**egg yolk**	1
3 tbsp	**amaretto or white crème de menthe (or orange juice)**	50 mL
4 tsp	**granulated sugar**	20 mL
2 cups	**sliced peaches**	500 mL
1 tbsp	**toasted slivered almonds**	15 mL

• In mixing bowl, beat ricotta until smooth. Add egg yolk, liqueur and sugar; mix well. Refrigerate until chilled.

• Place a few peach slices in each of 4 parfait glasses. Top with generous spoonful of ricotta mixture. Continue layering remaining peaches and ricotta mixture. Sprinkle with almonds. Makes 4 servings.

SOUFFLÉED DESSERT OMELETTE

Sweet omelettes are fast and easy; use any combination of fruit, and flavor them with whatever liqueur you like. Cook the omelettes just before serving.

2	eggs, separated	2
1 tbsp	granulated sugar	15 mL
1 tbsp	fruit liqueur	15 mL
1 tbsp	unsalted butter	15 mL
	Sweetened berries or sliced fruit	
	Icing sugar	

• In bowl, beat egg whites until stiff but not dry. In separate bowl, beat yolks with sugar and liqueur; fold into whites. Turn on broiler.
• In heavy ovenproof 8-inch (20 cm) skillet, melt butter; pour in egg mixture and spread evenly. Cook over medium-low heat, without stirring, until omelette is puffy and bottom is lightly browned, about 2 minutes. Broil about 8 inches (20 cm) from heat until top is lightly browned, about 2 minutes.
• Quickly spoon some berries over middle of omelette. With spatula, gently fold omelette in half to cover berries; slide out onto warm plate. Sift icing sugar over top and sprinkle with more berries. If desired, drizzle with more liqueur. Serve immediately. Makes 1 serving.

FRESH FRUIT IN YOGURT

When strawberries are in season, there's nothing better than dipping berries into sour cream or yogurt, then into brown sugar. In this easy version for winter, you can adjust the amount of fruit for your family so there are no leftovers.

1 cup	plain yogurt	250 mL
2 tbsp	packed brown sugar	25 mL
2 tbsp	toasted sliced almonds	25 mL
2	bananas	2
1	kiwifruit or 1 cup (250 mL) seedless green grapes, halved	1
1	ripe papaya or 3 nectarines	1

• Stir together yogurt, brown sugar and almonds; set aside.
• Peel and thickly slice bananas. Peel kiwifruit and thinly slice. Peel papaya and cut in half lengthwise; discard seeds. Slice papaya lengthwise; cut slices into bite-sized pieces. (If using nectarines, remove pits and slice.)
• In bowl, combine bananas, kiwifruit and papaya. Pour yogurt mixture over top and serve immediately. Makes 3 to 5 servings.

FROZEN FRUIT YOGURT

In food processor, combine 3 cups (750 mL) frozen fruit (peach slices or hulled strawberries) and 1/3 cup (75 mL) fruit/ berry sugar (instant dissolving sugar). Process until coarsely chopped. With machine running, gradually pour 1/2 cup (125 mL) plain yogurt through feed tube; process until smooth. Serve immediately. Makes about 3 cups (750 mL) or 4 servings.

FAST SAUCES FOR ICE CREAM

Choose one of these quick and easy sauces to turn plain ice cream into a wonderful dessert. Or simply drizzle your favorite liqueur over a scoop of vanilla ice cream.

BRANDIED CRANBERRY SAUCE:

1 cup	whole berry cranberry sauce	250 mL
1 tbsp	brandy (or 1 tsp/ 5 mL brandy extract)	15 mL

• Mix together cranberry sauce and brandy. Makes 1 cup (250 mL).

MINCEMEAT SAUCE:

1 cup	mincemeat (hot or cold)	250 mL
1 tbsp	rum (or 1 tsp/ 5 mL rum extract)	15 mL

• Mix together mincemeat and rum. Makes 1 cup (250 mL).

HOT CHERRY SAUCE:

1	can (14 oz/ 398 mL) pitted dark cherries	1
1/4 cup	packed brown sugar	50 mL
4 tsp	cornstarch	20 mL
2	drops almond extract	2

• Drain cherries, reserving syrup. In small saucepan, blend sugar and cornstarch. Stir in reserved cherry syrup. Cook, stirring, until mixture comes to full boil and thickens. Reduce heat to low; simmer for 2 minutes. Blend in almond extract; stir in cherries. Makes about 1-1/2 cups (375 mL).

Crème de Menthe drizzled over ice cream

CHOCOLATE FONDUE

In heavy saucepan, melt 4 oz (125 g) semisweet (bittersweet) chocolate and 1/2 cup (125 mL) light cream over low heat, stirring until smooth. Remove from heat; blend in 2 tbsp (25 mL) brandy, rum or liqueur. Transfer to fondue pot; set over warmer. Serve with bite-sized chunks of fresh fruit or pound cake. Makes 4 servings.

Keep several miniature liqueur bottles in your freezer (they won't freeze). Then for an easy dessert, pour a splash of your favorite ice-cold liqueur over refreshing ices or fresh fruit—simplicity at its best.

STRAWBERRIES AND SICILIAN CREAM

No one will guess this delicious dessert took only a few minutes to assemble.

1 cup	ricotta or cottage cheese	250 mL
1/4 cup	orange marmalade	50 mL
1 oz	semisweet chocolate, coarsely grated	30 g
1 tbsp	orange liqueur or orange juice	15 mL
2 cups	strawberries, hulled	500 mL

• In blender or food processor fitted with steel blade, process ricotta until smooth; add marmalade and process just until mixed.
• Transfer to bowl; stir in chocolate and liqueur. Cover and refrigerate until chilled.
• Divide strawberries among 4 goblets or dessert dishes; top each serving with ricotta-chocolate mixture. Makes 4 servings.

Easy Meal-Planner

Menus for everyday meals and casual entertaining

In this section we bring you 100 timesaving menus that mix and match recipes from this cookbook or offer suggestions for accompanying side dishes and desserts. Many of these meals can be prepared in 30 minutes or less. Don't forget to have your family help with the preparation and cooking.

EXPRESS LANE

FETTUCCINE WITH MUSHROOM AND CLAM SAUCE (p. 139)
FRENCH BREAD
CELERY AND OLIVES
SPEEDY MOUSSE (p. 15)

OPEN-FACED HAMBURGERS (p. 47)
DILL PICKLE STRIPS
SOUR CREAM FRUIT DIP (chart, p. 155)

SCALLOPS PROVENÇALE (p. 119)
RICE WITH BROCCOLI AND TOMATOES (p. 142)
DESSERT FRENCH TOAST (p. 152)

BRATWURST SKILLET SUPPER (p. 86)
PICKLED BEETS
RYE BREAD
FROSTED ANGEL CAKE (p. 156)

PORK CUTLETS WITH KIWI (p. 83)
JULIENNE OF CARROTS IN HONEY GLAZE (p. 151)
MELON BALLS WITH ICE CREAM

TURKEY CUTLETS WITH LEMON AND ROSEMARY (p. 107)
RICE PILAF (p. 143)
TOMATO WEDGES
FRESH FRUIT

*Lamb Patty in Pita Round
(p. 90)*

ONE-DISH DINNERS

SPEEDY LENTIL AND BEAN CASSEROLE (p. 140)
WHOLE WHEAT TOAST FINGERS
CARROT STICKS AND PICKLES
ORANGE-DRIZZLED CAKE SLICES (p. 155)

BEEF-CABBAGE SKILLET DINNER (p. 72)
SQUASH RINGS
BROILED SHERRIED GRAPEFRUIT (sidebar, p. 26)

BEEF NOODLE STOVE-TOP CASSEROLE (p. 74)
SLICED TOMATOES AND CUCUMBERS
DARK RYE BREAD
FROZEN FRUIT YOGURT (sidebar, p. 158)

VEGETABLE CHILI CHOWDER (p. 48)
MOZZARELLA TOASTS (p. 35)
FRESH FRUIT

RATATOUILLE AND CHICK-PEAS (p. 147)
MULTIGRAIN BREAD AND WHIPPED CREAM CHEESE
FRESH PINEAPPLE WEDGES AND COOKIES

SUCCOTASH STEW (p. 105)
GREENS WITH VINAIGRETTE (p. 22)
SHERBET AND COOKIES

JIFFY BEAN CASSEROLE (p. 146)
BREADSTICKS
PEPPER STRIPS
BANANAS AND MANDARIN ORANGES

LAMB HOT POT (p. 91)
FLUFFY RICE
GREENS WITH FETA CHEESE
GRAPES AND POUND CAKE

BEAT THE HEAT

CHILI BEEF BURGERS (p. 72)
COLESLAW (p. 64)
BERRIES AND CREAM

MUSTARD CHICKEN SAUTÉ (p. 98)
ORANGE, OLIVE AND ONION SALAD (p. 64)
FRUIT KABOBS (sidebar, p. 156)

CHILLED TOMATO BOUILLON (p. 13)
WARM STEAK SALAD (p. 66)
PEACH SLICES WITH BLUEBERRIES (chart, p. 155)

VEGETABLE COCKTAIL WITH CELERY
WARM MEXICAN SALAD (p. 63)
MELON CHUNKS WITH TEQUILA (chart, p. 155)

HERB-GRILLED TURKEY SCALLOPINI (p. 23)
GRILLED SEASONAL VEGETABLES
FRESH FRUIT IN YOGURT (p. 158)

PANTRY RAID

TOMATO BOUILLON (p. 13)
DOUBLE-OLIVE TUNA SPREAD ON HOVIS (p. 39)
RASPBERRY SHERBET WITH RASPBERRY SAUCE (sidebar, p. 156)

BAKED SALMON SALAD ON GREENS (p. 117)
MIXED OLIVES
MELBA TOAST
MANGO SLICES WITH LIME (chart, p. 155)

QUICK MACARONI AND CHEESE (p. 139)
VEGETABLE CRUDITÉS
BAKED WINTER COMPOTE (p. 24)

SPICY CLAMATO BISQUE (p. 55)
WARM CHEDDAR DIP (p. 37)
BREADSTICKS
BROILED BANANA SLICES (chart, p. 155)

TOMATO-BEAN CHOWDER (p. 50)
SPINACH DIP IN A RYE SHELL (p. 36)
PEACH AND RICOTTA PARFAIT (p. 157)

SALMON PAT-A-CAKES WITH QUICK TARTAR SAUCE (p. 110)
ORANGE-GLAZED BEETS (p. 149)
FRESH FRUIT

LIGHT AND BREEZY

LEMON-BASIL CHICKEN STRIPS (p. 20)
GREEN BEANS WITH GARLIC AND SESAME SEEDS (p. 146)
LIME SHERBET AND ANGEL FOOD CAKE SLICES

LAMB CHOPS WITH HONEY-SOY GLAZE (p. 88)
CARAWAY VEGETABLE PLATTER (sidebar, p. 88)
KIWI SLICES WITH BLUEBERRIES

SKILLET CHICKEN SALAD (p. 62)
PARMESAN TOASTS (p. 9)
GHERKINS
CARAMELIZED ORANGES (chart, p. 155)

DELICATE SALMON CHOWDER WITH PASTA SHELLS (p. 57)
ROMAINE AND RED ONION SALAD (p. 26)
CRACKERS
WHOLE STRAWBERRIES WITH WHIPPED CREAM CHEESE

LEMON SHRIMP WITH FRESH VEGETABLES (p. 116)
ENGLISH MUFFINS
BLACK OLIVES
ORANGE AND GRAPEFRUIT SECTIONS

LINGUINE AND FETTUCCINE WITH SPRING LEEKS AND ZUCCHINI (p. 138)
WHOLE WHEAT CRACKERS
STRAWBERRIES IN WHITE WINE

CHICKEN AND APPLE SAUTÉ (p. 99)
TOASTED PITAS
VEGETABLE CRUDITÉS
YOGURT SUNDAES (chart, p. 155)

MONDAY-TO-FRIDAY SUPPERS

BANGERS WITH ONIONS AND APPLES (p. 85)
BUTTERED NOODLES
MUSTARD PICKLES
PEACHES AND OATMEAL COOKIES

HURRY CURRY (p. 80)
ORANGE RICE AND RED LENTIL PILAF (p. 143)
CUCUMBER SLICES IN YOGURT
SHERBET

MINI MEAT LOAVES (p. 68)
ROMAINE AND PEPPER SALAD
TOASTED BAGEL WEDGES
ICE CREAM WITH MINCEMEAT SAUCE (p. 159)

CREOLE HAM AND RICE (p. 80)
CELERY AND CARROT STICKS
BANANA SLICES WITH TOASTED COCONUT

POTATO-ZUCCHINI PANCAKES WITH SOUR CREAM (p. 150)
MIXED LETTUCES WITH HERB VINAIGRETTE (p. 22)
FRESH FRUIT IN SEASON

SAUSAGE PATTIES WITH MUSTARD CREAM (p. 87)
STEAMED MIXED VEGETABLES
ORANGE SLICES WITH FAST CHOCOLATE SAUCE (p. 31)

OMELETTES TO ORDER (p. 19)
TOAST FINGERS
TOMATO WEDGES
ICE CREAM WITH HOT CHERRY SAUCE (p. 159)

SOLE WITH BLACK BUTTER (p. 113)
PARSLEY-LEMON RICE (p. 140)
CHERRY TOMATOES AND CUCUMBER SPEARS
MELON CHUNKS

PASTA POWER

SPAGHETTI WITH SAUSAGE AND TOMATO SAUCE (p. 133)
MIXED GREENS WITH CROUTONS
FRESH FIGS

TWO-PEPPER PASTA WITH PROSCIUTTO (p. 136)
GREENS WITH PARMESAN AND ITALIAN-FLAVORED VINAIGRETTE (p. 22)
HONEYDEW AND CANTALOUPE CHUNKS

WARM PASTA SEAFOOD SALAD (p. 61)
POPPYSEED BAGELS
PEAR HALVES WITH MASCARPONE AND HAZELNUTS

FUSILLI WITH TOMATO-VEGETABLE PRIMAVERA (p. 137)
MARINATED MUSHROOMS OR ARTICHOKE HEARTS
BREADSTICKS
STRAWBERRIES AND SICILIAN CREAM (p. 159)

ROTINI WITH SALMON AND CHIVES (p. 133)
MEDITERRANEAN SALAD (p. 67)
ORANGE SLICES WITH POMEGRANATE SEEDS

PENNE WITH SWEET PEPPERS AND TWO CHEESES (p. 136)
HEARTS OF ROMAINE AND CUCUMBER SALAD (p. 59)
ICED WATERMELON

COMPANY PLEASERS

MEDALLIONS OF LAMB IN RED WINE SAUCE (p. 27)
BULGUR AND MUSHROOM PILAF (p. 28)
GREENS WITH TOMATO VINAIGRETTE (p. 22)
BERRIES WITH CREAM

ALMOND-BREADED FILLETS (p. 112)
GREEN BEAN AND CELERY SAUTÉ (p. 144)
CRUSTY ROLLS
ORANGES IN COINTREAU (chart, p. 155)

PORK MEDALLIONS WITH CRANBERRY-PORT SAUCE (p. 84)
SAVORY VEGETABLE RING (p. 144)
PEAR SLICES WITH CAMBOZOLA AND WALNUTS (chart, p. 155)

OVEN-POACHED SALMON IN DILL SAUCE (p. 111)
ASPARAGUS AND BUTTON MUSHROOM STIR-FRY (p. 149)
PUMPERNICKEL BREAD
FRESH PINEAPPLE SPEARS WITH ICE CREAM

BEEF PAILLARDS WITH DOUBLE PEPPER SAUCE (p. 71)
BROCCOLI SALAD WITH SUNFLOWER SEEDS (p. 61)
APPLESAUCE ANGEL PUDDING (p. 152)

PORK TENDERLOIN WITH MUSTARD-PEPPERCORN CRUST (p. 81)
PARSLEY-LEMON ORZO (p. 140)
STEAMED CARROTS AND SNOW PEAS
ICE CREAM WITH BRANDIED CRANBERRY SAUCE (p. 159)

CHICKEN BREASTS WITH CHÈVRE AND JULIENNE PEPPERS (p. 107)
SUGARSNAP PEAS
STRAWBERRIES ROMANOFF (chart, p. 155)

SCHNITZELLED VEAL CHOPS (p. 92)
NOODLES WITH POPPY SEEDS
GREENS WITH CREAMY DRESSING (p. 22)
APPLE AND PEAR WEDGES

SNACK ATTACK

THREE-PEPPER THREE-CHEESE PIZZA (p. 32)
OLIVES AND ARTICHOKES

BANANA BUTTERMILK PANCAKES (p. 37)
BACON STRIPS
MAPLE SYRUP

TACOS WITH TOMATO AND CUCUMBER SALSA (p. 40)
STRAWBERRIES WITH CREAM

SPICY TOMATO JUICE
MUSHROOM AND MOZZARELLA PIZZA (p. 42)

SCRAMBLED EGGS IN A PITA (p. 124)
FRESH VEGETABLE STICKS

REAL WELSH RAREBIT (p. 129)
TOAST TRIANGLES
GREENS WITH TOMATO DRESSING (p. 22)

CREAMY BLUE CHEESE DIP (p. 37)
FLATBREAD
BROCCOLI SALAD WITH SUNFLOWER SEEDS (p. 61)

CHICKEN HASH (p. 97)
TOASTED ENGLISH MUFFINS
ORANGES IN COINTREAU (chart, p. 155)

CHEDDAR-SOUFFLÉ OMELETTE (p. 129)
SAUTÉED CHERRY TOMATOES WITH FRESH BASIL (p. 149)
PLUMS OR NECTARINES

FISH FILLETS IN PACKETS (p. 110)
GREEN BEANS WITH ALMONDS
SPEEDY MOUSSE (p. 15)

MUSSELS WITH GARLIC AND TOMATOES (p. 119)
CRUSTY FRENCH BREAD
MELON SLICES WITH FRESH FIGS

TOMATO LINGUINE WITH SALMON (p. 132)
GREENS WITH ITALIAN-FLAVORED VINAIGRETTE (p. 22)
FRESH PEACHES WITH BROWN SUGAR

HEARTY CRAB VICHYSSOISE (p. 57)
PARMESAN TOASTS (p. 9)

HOT CRAB AND AVOCADO SALAD ON CROISSANTS (p. 60)
ICED COFFEE

GOOD FOR YOU

CHILI WITH CHICK-PEAS (p. 72)
MOZZARELLA TOASTS (p. 35)
ROMAINE AND RED ONION SALAD (p. 26)
FRESH FRUIT

BABY BEEF LIVER WITH YOGURT-MUSTARD SAUCE (p. 75)
TOMATO SLICES AND CARROT STICKS
ORANGE-DRIZZLED CAKE SLICES (p. 155)

SCALLOPS AND BROCCOLI WITH ALMONDS (p. 117)
BULGUR AND MUSHROOM PILAF (p. 28)
SLICED TOMATOES
PEARS AND GRAPES

CITRUS SALMON SALAD (p. 62)
SESAME BREADSTICKS
SHERBET AND WAFER COOKIES

SCHNITZELLED PORK CHOPS (p. 92)
COLESLAW WITH APPLES (p. 64)
YOGURT SUNDAES (chart, p. 155)

FILLET OF SOLE WITH GREEN GRAPES (p. 113)
FLUFFY RICE WITH PEAS
FRESH FRUIT IN YOGURT (p. 158)

FOR THE LUNCH BUNCH

LAMB PATTIES IN PITA ROUNDS (p. 90)
CRISP CRUDITÉS
FRUIT AND COOKIES

CRAB SALAD CROISSANTS WITH PEACHES AND PECANS (p. 38)
APPLE AND PEAR SLICES WITH CHEESE

MUFFULETTAS (p. 43)
BARTLETT PEARS AND GINGERSNAPS

LEAN BEEF SUPER SUPPER SANDWICHES (p. 45)
GREENS WITH CLASSIC VINAIGRETTE (p. 22)

OPEN-FACED STEAK SANDWICH WITH MUSHROOM SAUCE (p. 47)
GREEN ONIONS
STUFFED OLIVES
CHOCOLATE-DRIZZLED CAKE SLICES

BEAN AND BACON SOUP (p. 50)
GARLIC TOMATO CROSTINI (p. 34)
BOSC PEARS

CHILLED CUCUMBER SOUP (p. 55)
PIZZA BREAD (p. 42)
FROSTED GRAPES (p. 28)

CALIFORNIA STUFFED ZUCCHINI (p. 148)
GRAINY BREAD AND WHIPPED CREAM CHEESE
FLAVORED YOGURT

ORIENTAL EXPRESS

STIR-FRIED BEEF WITH BROCCOLI (p. 71)
STEAMED RICE
LETTUCE WEDGES WITH CREAMY DRESSING (p. 22)
ORANGE SLICES WITH GINGERSNAP CRUMBS

CHICKEN AND RED PEPPER STIR-FRY (p. 94)
RICE VERMICELLI
CELERY HEARTS
ICE CREAM COOKIE SANDWICHES

BEEF TERIYAKI WITH SWEET-AND-SOUR VEGETABLES (p. 77)
NOODLES AND DIPPING SAUCES (sidebar, p. 77)
GRAPES
FORTUNE COOKIES

EIGHT TREASURE SOUP (p. 55)
GREENS WITH SMOKED SALMON
RICE CAKES
FRESH BERRIES

ORIENTAL HOT POT (p. 118)
SESAME CRACKERS
SHERBET AND CHOCOLATE WAFER COOKIES

ORIENTAL FISH FILLETS (p. 108)
ASPARAGUS AND BUTTON MUSHROOM STIR-FRY (p. 149)
ORANGE SECTIONS WITH LICHEE NUTS

MEATLESS MEALS

GNOCCHI WITH FOUR CHEESES (p. 135)
SESAME CRACKERS
WATERCRESS AND RED ONION SALAD
FRESH FIGS WITH FLAVORED CREAM (chart, p. 155)

TOMATO MUSHROOM SOUP WITH RYE CROUTONS (p. 56)
ARTICHOKE SALAD IN ROMAINE BOATS (p. 58)
PINEAPPLE SPEARS

MUSHROOM CONSOMMÉ (sidebar, p. 52)
AVOCADO AND WALNUT SALAD (p. 67)
CHEESE WITH FRUIT

AVOCADO MELTS (p. 46)
OLIVES
SAUTÉED APPLE SLICES (chart, p. 155)

COUNTRY GARDEN POACHED EGGS (p. 127)
SESAME PITA ROUNDS
BERRIES WITH SOUR CREAM AND BROWN SUGAR

FRITTATA IN A SKILLET (p. 122)
PUMPERNICKEL BREAD
CHOCOLATE FONDUE (sidebar, p. 159)

QUICK CLASSICS WITH A TWIST

CURRIED SQUASH SOUP (p. 54)
SIRLOIN STEAK WITH WINE AND SHALLOT SAUCE (p. 70)
GREEN AND RED CABBAGE WITH POPPYSEED VINAIGRETTE
ICED GRAPES WITH YOGURT

LIGHT EGGS BENEDICT WITH PROSCIUTTO (p. 123)
LETTUCE AND ENDIVE SALAD
LEMON SHERBET WITH CASSIS

ROESTI POTATOES WITH POACHED EGGS (p. 126)
RADISHES AND OLIVES
PEACH AND RICOTTA PARFAIT (p. 157)

SPICED TOMATO JUICE
CROQUE-MONSIEUR (p. 45)
APPLESAUCE WITH NUTS AND CINNAMON

FRENCH TOAST WITH PESTO (p. 38)
CUCUMBER CHUNKS WITH CLASSIC VINAIGRETTE (p. 22)
RASPBERRIES WITH CRÈME FRAÎCHE

VEAL SCALLOPS WITH LEEKS AND LEMON MARMALADE (p. 14)
PASTA SHELLS WITH RED PEPPER AND PARSLEY SAUCE (p. 130)
TOSSED GREENS WITH VINAIGRETTE (p. 22)
MANGO SLICES WITH WHIPPED CREAM AND CANDIED GINGER

Tips for the Rush-Hour Cook

Creative rush-hour cooking is easy when you keep a well-stocked kitchen. Be prepared: take full advantage of your supply cupboards, refrigerator and freezer. With enough basics and even a few gourmet treats on hand, you can cook for family and guests without frequent trips to the grocery store.

The list of items we've included here is extensive and you may not have the space to store all of them. They are simply suggestions—you can choose the assortment that suits your own style of cooking or add your own favorite ingredients. Our tips for organizing your pantry will keep you from wasting valuable time searching for items.

Organization

Keep track of the items on hand by organizing cupboards, refrigerator and freezer.

Cupboards:

• Group foods together. Reserve one section or an entire cupboard for cans, one for crackers, pasta and other dry foods, one shelf for vinegars, oils, soy sauce, etc.
• Buy spices in small quantities; date them and use within one year. Store them alphabetically in a dry cool place for easy access.

Refrigerator and Freezer:

• A written list beside your freezer is handy; check each item off as used.
• Label and date items using moistureproof stick-on tabs or masking tape and waterproof marking pens.
• Routinely do a check of freezer and refrigerator for forgotten or outdated items.

The Rush-Hour Pantry

• Oils and Vinegars: A good vegetable oil for cooking and salads like corn or canola and a specialty oil like extra-virgin olive oil or walnut oil; white and cider vinegars, and red and white wine vinegars or specialty vinegars (fruit or herb).
• Pasta, rice and grains: Assorted pasta shapes; bulgur; couscous; long-grain white rice and Arborio rice; canned beans such as kidney, lima, chick-peas and lentils.

• Stocks: Beef and chicken stocks, consommé.
• Herbs and spices: Fresh herbs whenever possible, or dried: sage, rosemary, thyme, basil, oregano, tarragon; cumin, hot pepper flakes, chili powder, saffron, paprika, cayenne pepper and peppercorns; cinnamon, ginger, nutmeg and cloves.
• Staples: Flours (all-purpose, whole wheat); sugars (granulated, brown, icing); honey and maple syrup; unflavored gelatin; cream of tartar, baking soda and baking powder; cornstarch; extracts (vanilla and almond);

cocoa, chocolate (unsweetened and bittersweet) blocks and chips; assorted dried fruits.
• Canned or bottled products: Tomato paste and tomato sauce; salmon, tuna, anchovies, clams; fruits (pears, pineapple, peaches); vegetables (tomatoes, beets, small potatoes, yams); marinated artichokes, mushrooms and olives; pickles (sweet and dill); soy sauce; teriyaki sauce, salsa, Worcestershire sauce and hot pepper sauce; preserves (jams, jellies, chutneys); water chestnuts, capers and jalapeño peppers; wines and liqueurs for cooking.
• Special occasion shelf: Smoked oysters, canned lobster or crab; black (lumpfish), red (salmon) and golden (whitefish) caviars; roasted peppers, sun-dried tomatoes, pesto sauce, antipasto, olive paste, anchovy paste, dried mushrooms; lemon curd; amaretti cookies, macaroons and other special cookies.
• Crackers, breadsticks, melba toast, croutons, rice cakes.
• Garlic.

The Rush-Hour Refrigerator

• Milk, sour cream, yogurt and butter.
• Eggs.
• Cheeses: Parmesan, Swiss, Cheddar and cream cheese.
• Mayonnaise or salad dressings, prepared horseradish, Dijon and other mustards.
• Vegetables: Carrots, celery, green and red peppers, potatoes, onions, green onions, salad greens, chives, leeks.

• Fruits: Apples, lemons, limes and oranges.
• Nuts: Walnuts, almonds and pecans.
• Parsley and other fresh herbs (when available).
• Maple syrup.

The Rush-Hour Freezer

• Fruit: Raspberries, strawberries, blueberries; juice concentrates.
• Vegetables of your choice.

- Pastas: Fresh, if desired; tortellini and ravioli.
- Boneless chicken breasts, turkey scallopini.
- Fish: Individually frozen boneless fillets.

- Breads and rolls; fresh bread crumbs.
- Ice cream and sherbets.
- Bakery items: Pastry shells, pre-made pizza rounds; lady fingers, macaroons, sugar cookies, vanilla wafers, gingersnaps, chocolate wafers; sponge cake rounds (layers), pound cake, angel food cake.
- Shredded Cheddar cheese.
- Grated Parmesan cheese in tightly covered container.

EXTRA TIPS FOR THE BUSY COOK

Planning Tactics

- Plan ahead. Visualize the steps involved in making a dish. If you think it through beforehand, you'll have a picture in your mind of what needs to be done.
- As soon as you arrive home, turn on the oven if you're going to use it. Start by preparing the dish that takes the longest time to make.
- Label the bottoms of pans, casseroles and baking dishes with an indelible marker to make it easy to find a specific size.
- Take a recipe with you to work and shop for ingredients at lunch-time or on your way home.
- Simplify your menus—one really good dish with easy accompaniments is sufficient.
- Do whatever you can the night before or before leaving for work. Every little bit helps.

Get All The Help You Can

- Enlist the help of family members or guests. Even pre-schoolers can set the table, put rolls in a basket and fill the napkin-holder.
- Go for the gadgets—if they save time and effort. An egg slicer, strawberry huller, zester (to remove grated rind from lemons, limes and oranges), stripper (to cut a strip of lemon peel), and a good vegetable peeler are invaluable.
- Learn to use your food processor. Save precious time by knowing what it does best and how.
- Keep kitchen equipment in good working order. Sharp knives cut best; mixers need oiling.
- Use kitchen shears to snip herbs, open packages and cut up chicken.
- Let your microwave help. Measure, mix and microwave in a large microwaveable measuring cup. Melt butter, cheese and chocolate in the microwave. Prepare or reheat sauces quickly. Microwave vegetables in a hurry. Partially cook meats or poultry in the microwave and then finish them on the grill or under the broiler.

Advance Preparation

- Buy staples once a month and fruits and vegetables once a week.
- Clean and dry vegetables when you purchase them to have ready for quick cooking.
- Buy foods in portion sizes, such as chicken breasts, chops and fish fillets. Individual portions cook quickest.
- Take advantage of supermarket specials and buy tender cuts of meat for quick cooking.
- Freeze boneless chicken breasts individually. Place the pieces on a baking sheet in the freezer until frozen. Wrap each one in plastic wrap, sealing well. Label and freeze for up to six months.
- Grate the leftovers of cheese and store in airtight plastic bags in the freezer. Grate and add additional bits of cheese as they accumulate. Use frozen grated cheese to top broiled meats, casseroles and steamed vegetables.
- Keep a supply of bread crumbs on hand. Process crusts of fresh bread in the blender or food processor. Store in a plastic bag in the freezer.
- If you love bacon: Cook bacon until crisp; drain on paper towels, crumble and freeze. Reheat quickly in skillet or microwave or sprinkle frozen bacon bits on casseroles before baking.
- If you use a lot of garlic: Peel garlic cloves; cover whole or chopped cloves with olive oil and store in a covered jar in the refrigerator for up to 3 months (1/2 tsp/2 mL of minced garlic is approximately equal to one clove).
- If you stir-fry frequently: Finely chop or sliver fresh gingerroot, cover with sherry and store in a small covered jar in the refrigerator for up to 6 months.
- When preparing more than one recipe, check each to see if any steps or ingredients are duplicated. Then, if you need chopped onions in two recipes, you can do them all at once and save time.

Quick Cooking Tips

- Peel whole small onions quickly: Plunge them into boiling water for 2 to 3 minutes. Drain and rinse under cold water before peeling. The skins will slip off easily.
- Peel garlic quickly: Place a clove on a flat surface and hit it with flat side of a heavy knife. The peel will come off easily.
- Peel tomatoes easily: Plunge them into boiling water for about 1 minute. Refresh under cold water before peeling.
- To chop canned tomatoes: Use 2 knives or even kitchen scissors right in the measuring cup.
- Make sauce in a hurry: Deglaze the pan that you cook meat in with a little wine, while the pan is still hot. Using a wooden spoon, scrape up any brown bits in bottom of pan. Boil liquid until reduced and thickened.
- To make 1/2 cup (125 mL) fresh bread crumbs: Tear 1 slice of bread into pieces; whirl in blender or food processor on high speed.
- If a recipe calls for just part of a can of tomato paste, freeze the remainder. Drop tablespoonfuls (15 mL) onto foil-lined baking sheet. Freeze, then transfer frozen chunks (already measured) to a plastic bag.
- Meat loaf is great, but it does take a long time to bake. Individual loaves or small rounds baked in muffin tins take less time to cook.
- Save the drained marinade from marinated artichokes to use as a flavorful vinaigrette.
- Substitute dried herbs for fresh or fresh for dried in a recipe. The rule of thumb is 1 tsp (5 mL) dried for 1 tbsp (15 mL) chopped fresh.

Acknowledgments and Credits

THE CONTRIBUTORS

The names of the contributing food writers are included with the recipe titles in this index for your easy reference. The recipes are organized by page number.

RECIPE TITLE	CONTRIBUTOR	PAGE
Rosemary and Mustard Glazed Chicken	Patricia Jamieson	11
Tomato Bouillon	Bonnie Cowan	13
Parmesan Fish Fingers with Lemon	Bonnie Cowan	13
Veal Scallops with Leeks and Lemon Marmalade	Bonnie Cowan	14
Speedy Mousse	Margaret Fraser	15
Fondue with Italian Flavors	Bonnie Cowan	16
Antipasto Platter	Bonnie Cowan	17
Basic French Omelette	Elizabeth Baird	19
Lemon-Basil Chicken Strips	Kay Spicer	20
Herb-Grilled Turkey Scallopini	Anne Lindsay	23
Baked Winter Compote	Margaret Fraser	24
Zucchini, Potato and Egg Skillet Supper	Anne Lindsay	25
Romaine and Red Onion Salad	Margaret Fraser	26
Medallions of Lamb in Red Wine Sauce	Iris Raven	27
Bulgur and Mushroom Pilaf	Anne Lindsay	28
Chicken and Snow Peas in Packets	Bonnie Cowan	31
Fast Chocolate Sauce	Margaret Fraser	31
Three-Pepper Three-Cheese Pizza	Carol Ferguson	32
Hummus	Anne Lindsay	34
Garlic Tomato Crostini	Elizabeth Baird	34
Mozzarella Toasts	Bonnie Cowan	35
Creamy Blue Cheese Dip	Kay Spicer	37
Banana Buttermilk Pancakes	Bonnie Stern	37
French Toast with Pesto	Patricia Jamieson	38
Crab Salad Croissants with Peaches and Pecans	Carol Ferguson	38
Double-Olive Tuna Spread	Bonnie Cowan	39
Tacos with Tomato and Cucumber Salsa	Anne Lindsay	40
Mushroom and Mozzarella Pizza	Anne Lindsay	42
Pizza Bread	Beth Moffatt	42
Muffulettas	Bonnie Stern	43
Croque-Monsieur	Beth Moffatt	45
Lean Beef Super Supper Sandwiches	Iris Raven	45
Avocado Melts	Beth Moffatt	46
Open-Faced Hamburgers	Margaret Fraser	47
Open-Faced Steak Sandwich with Mushroom Sauce	Bonnie Cowan	47
Bean and Bacon Soup	Bonnie Cowan	50
Tomato-Bean Chowder	Anne Lindsay	50
Hearty Ham and Vegetable Bean Soup	Anne Lindsay	51
Clam and Corn Chowder	Margaret Fraser	52
Curried Cauliflower and Tofu Soup	Rose Murray	52
Mushroom Consommé	Iris Raven	52
Cream of Vegetable Soup	Iris Raven	53
Broccoli and Red Onion Soup	Bonnie Stern	54
Eight Treasure Soup	Iris Raven	55
Spicy Clamato Bisque	Beth Moffatt	55
Chilled Cucumber Soup	Carol Ferguson	55
Spa Vegetable Soup	Anne Lindsay	56
Tomato Mushroom Soup with Rye Croutons	Elizabeth Baird	56
Delicate Salmon Chowder with Pasta Shells	Elizabeth Baird	57
Hearty Crab Vichyssoise	Beth Moffatt	57
Artichoke Salad in Romaine Boats	Iris Raven	58
Carrot, Celery and Pecan Salad	Iris Raven	59
Curly Endive with Walnuts and Blue Cheese	Elizabeth Baird	59
Hearts of Romaine and Cucumber Salad	Bonnie Cowan	59
Hot Crab and Avocado Salad	Beth Moffatt	60
Cucumber Salad with Yogurt and Dill	Bonnie Cowan	60
Warm Pasta Seafood Salad	Carol Ferguson	61
Broccoli Salad with Sunflower Seeds	Anne Lindsay	61
Citrus Salmon Salad	Beth Moffatt	62
Skillet Chicken Salad	Rose Murray	62

RECIPE TITLE	CONTRIBUTOR	PAGE
Warm Mexican Salad	Margaret Fraser	63
Orange, Olive and Onion Salad	Anne Lindsay	64
Romaine Salad with Caesar Dressing	Carol Ferguson	64
Coleslaw	Anne Lindsay	64
Mediterranean Salad	Carol Ferguson	67
Spinach and Romaine Salad with Horseradish Dressing	Bonnie Cowan	67
Avocado and Walnut Salad	Anne Lindsay	67
Mini Meat Loaves	Margaret Fraser	68
Stir-Fried Beef with Broccoli	Rose Murray	71
Beef Paillards with Double Pepper Sauce	Bonnie Stern	71
Beef-Cabbage Skillet Dinner	Rose Murray	72
Chili with Chick-Peas	Anne Lindsay	72
Chili Beef Burgers	Elizabeth Baird	72
Blue Cheese Burgers	Rose Murray	73
Beef Noodle Stove-Top Casserole	Carol Ferguson	74
Baby Beef Liver with Yogurt-Mustard Sauce	Anne Lindsay	75
Beef Teriyaki with Sweet-and-Sour Vegetables	Iris Raven	77
Cheese-Topped Pork Chops	Rose Murray	77
One Potato—Two Potato and Chops	Kay Spicer	78
Pork Chops in Beer with Sauerkraut	Carol Ferguson	78
Hurry Curry	Kay Spicer	80
Creole Ham and Rice	Kay Spicer	80
Pork Chops with Pink Pears	Margaret Fraser	82
Pork and Red Pepper Shish Kabobs	Bonnie Stern	83
Pork Cutlets with Kiwi	Margaret Fraser	83
Pork Medallions with Cranberry-Port Sauce	Beth Moffatt	84
Bangers with Onions and Apples	Kay Spicer	85
Pork Tenderloin with Mustard and Herbs	Anne Lindsay	85
Lamb Chops Creole	Beth Moffatt	88
Grilled Lamb Chops with Herb Butter	Anne Lindsay	90
Lamb Patties in Pita Rounds	Anne Lindsay	90
Lamb Hot Pot	Kay Spicer	91
Schnitzelled Chops or Chicken	Carol Ferguson	92
Veal Scallopini in Mushroom Madeira Sauce	Carol Ferguson	92
Veal Chops with Green Peppercorns	Bonnie Stern	93
Stir-Fried Chicken and Snow Peas	Bonnie Stern	96
Saucy Chicken with Green Onions	Anne Lindsay	96
Chicken Hash	Bonnie Stern	97
Lemon Chicken	Anne Lindsay	98
Chicken and Apple Sauté	Beth Moffatt	99
Sunny Citrus Chicken	Carol Ferguson	100
Italian-Style Chicken	Carol Ferguson	101
Tropical Chicken	Carol Ferguson	101
Coriander-Crumbed Chicken Wings and Potato Wedges	Kay Spicer	102
Raspberry Chicken	Bonnie Cowan	102
Succotash Stew	Kay Spicer	105
Chicken Breasts Piccata	Bonnie Stern	105
Chicken Breasts with Chèvre and Julienne Peppers	Bonnie Stern	107
Turkey Cutlets with Lemon and Rosemary	Bonnie Stern	107
Fish Fillets in Packets	Anne Lindsay	110
Salmon Pat-a-Cakes with Quick Tartar Sauce	Margaret Fraser	110
Oven-Poached Salmon in Dill Sauce	Patricia Jamieson	111
Almond-Breaded Fillets	Anne Lindsay	112
Sole with Black Butter	Anne Lindsay	113
Fillet of Sole with Green Grapes	Anne Lindsay	113
Baked Haddock Fillets with Cheese	Iris Raven	113
Fish Fillets with Lime-Ginger Sauce	Bonnie Cowan	114
Lemon Shrimp with Fresh Vegetables	Kay Spicer	116
Scallops and Broccoli with Almonds	Margaret Fraser	117
Baked Salmon Salad	Margaret Fraser	117
Oriental Hot Pot	Kay Spicer	118

RECIPE TITLE	CONTRIBUTOR	PAGE
Scallops Provençale	Bonnie Stern	119
Watercress Frittata	Rose Murray	120
Frittata in a Skillet	Margaret Fraser	122
Bacon and Swiss Cheese Frittata	Elizabeth Baird	122
Light Eggs Benedict with Prosciutto	Rose Murray	123
Spanish Tortilla	Bonnie Stern	125
Individual Three-Cheese Soufflés	Margaret Fraser	126
Roesti Potatoes with Poached Eggs	Patricia Jamieson	126
Country Garden Poached Eggs	Kay Spicer	127
Mock Cheese Soufflé	Elizabeth Baird	128
Real Welsh Rarebit	Kay Spicer	129
Cheddar-Soufflé Omelette	Elizabeth Baird	129
Pasta Shells with Red Pepper and Parsley Sauce	Patricia Jamieson	130
Tomato Linguine with Salmon	Iris Raven	132
Rotini with Salmon and Chives	Anne Lindsay	133
Spaghetti with Sausage and Tomato Sauce	Carol Ferguson	133
Broccoli Pasta	Anne Lindsay	134
Gnocchi with Four Cheeses	Iris Raven	135
Spaghetti Carbonara	Carol Ferguson	135
Penne with Sweet Peppers and Two Cheeses	Rose Murray	136
Two-Pepper Pasta with Prosciutto	Iris Raven	136
Linguine and Fettuccine with Spring Leeks and Zucchini	Anne Lindsay	138
Fettuccine with Mushroom and Clam Sauce	Carol Ferguson	139
Quick Macaroni and Cheese	Anne Lindsay	139
Parsley-Lemon Orzo	Carol Ferguson	140
Speedy Lentil and Bean Casserole	Anne Lindsay	140
Pasta with Artichokes and Pine Nuts	Margaret Fraser	141
Pasta with Chick-Peas	Elizabeth Baird	142
Rice with Broccoli and Tomatoes	Bonnie Cowan	142
Rice Pilaf	Bonnie Stern	143
Savory Vegetable Ring	Bonnie Cowan	144
Green Bean and Celery Sauté	Anne Lindsay	144
Green Beans with Garlic and Sesame Seeds	Anne Lindsay	146
Jiffy Bean Casserole	Anne Lindsay	146
Vegetable Sauté	Anne Lindsay	146
Ratatouille and Chick-Peas	Kay Spicer	147
California Stuffed Zucchini	Kay Spicer	148
Sautéed Cherry Tomatoes with Fresh Basil	Bonnie Cowan	149
Asparagus and Button Mushroom Stir-Fry	Elizabeth Baird	149
Potato-Zucchini Pancakes	Bonnie Cowan	150
Jarlsberg and Green Beans in Mustard Vinaigrette	Elizabeth Baird	151
Fried Tomatoes	Bonnie Stern	151
Julienne of Carrots in Honey Glaze	Bonnie Cowan	151
Applesauce Angel Pudding	Margaret Fraser	152
Dessert French Toast	Margaret Fraser	152
Orange-Drizzled Cake Slices	Margaret Fraser	155
Frosted Angel Cake	Margaret Fraser	156
Stove-Top Rice Pudding	Bonnie Cowan	156
Peach and Ricotta Parfait	Bonnie Cowan	157
Souffléed Dessert Omelette	Carol Ferguson	158
Fresh Fruit in Yogurt	Rose Murray	158
Fast Sauces for Ice Cream	Margaret Fraser	159
Strawberries and Sicilian Cream	Kay Spicer	159

The remaining recipes in this cookbook, as well as the handy charts and hints, were developed in the *Canadian Living* test kitchen by test kitchen manager **Patricia Jamieson** and her staff. Special thanks to staff member **Janet Cornish**.

PHOTOGRAPHY CREDITS

Fred Bird: front, front flap and back of jacket; pages 7, 9, 10, 12, 15, 17, 18, 21, 23, 25, 27, 29, 30, 33, 35, 36, 39, 41, 43, 44, 46, 49, 51, 53, 54, 56, 58, 60, 63, 66, 69, 70, 73, 75, 76, 79, 82, 84, 85, 91, 93, 97, 99, 100, 103, 104, 111, 112, 116, 118, 121, 123–25, 127, 128, 131, 132, 134, 137, 138, 141, 142, 145, 147, 148, 150, 153, 154, 157, 159, 160.

Christopher Campbell: back flap of jacket.

Nino D'Angelo: page 95.

Michael Kohn: pages 106, 115.

Nancy Shanoff: pages 81, 89.

Mike Visser: pages 65, 109.

Stanley Wong: page 158.

Food Stylists: **Margaret Fraser**
Jennifer McLagan
Olga Truchan

Props Coordinator: **Debby Boyden**

The publisher would also like to thank the following for the use of props for photography:

Grant's China: pages 25, 27, 39, 43, 44, 60, 69, 75, 93, 145, 148, 150, 154, 157.
John Somers Pewter: pages 150 (fork and knife); 154 (fork).

Illustrator: **Wesley Lowe**

Index

A

Almond-Breaded Fillets, 112
Angel Cake, Frosted, 156
Antipasto Platter, 17
Appetizers
    Antipasto Platter, 17
    Double-Olive Tuna Spread, 39
    Garlic Tomato Crostini, 34
    Hummus, 34
    Mozzarella Toasts, 35
    Parmesan Toasts, 9
    Spinach Dip in a Rye Shell, 36
Apple
    Bangers with Onions and Apples, 85
    Sauté, Chicken and, 99
    Slices, Sautéed, 155
Applesauce Angel Pudding, 152
Artichoke Salad in Romaine Boats, 58
Asparagus and Button Mushroom Stir-Fry, 149
Avocado and Walnut Salad, 67
Avocado Melts, 46
Avocado Salad, Hot Crab and, 60

B

Baby Beef Liver with Yogurt-Mustard Sauce, 75
Bacon
    and Egg Salad, Warm, 65
    and Swiss Cheese Frittata, 122
    Scrambled Eggs with Tomato, Basil and, 124
    Soup, Bean and, 50
Baked Haddock Fillets with Cheese, 113
Baked Salmon Salad, 117
Baked Whitefish with Mustard-Dill Sauce, 114
Baked Winter Compote, 24
Banana
    Boats, Barbecued, 155
    Buttermilk Pancakes, 37
Bangers with Onions and Apples, 85
Barbecued Banana Boats, 155
Basic French Omelette, 19

Beans
    Bean and Bacon Soup, 50
    Chowder, Tomato, 50
    Hearty Ham and Vegetable Bean Soup, 51
    Jarlsberg and Green Beans in Mustard Vinaigrette, 151
    Jiffy Bean Casserole, 146
    Speedy Lentil and Bean Casserole, 140
Beef
    Baby Beef Liver with Yogurt-Mustard Sauce, 75
    Beef-Cabbage Skillet Dinner, 72
    Beef Noodle Stove-Top Casserole, 74
    Beef Paillards with Double Pepper Sauce, 71
    Beef Teriyaki with Sweet-and-Sour Vegetables, 77
    Blue Cheese Burgers, 73
    Burgers with Sour Cream Sauce, 72
    Chili Beef Burgers, 72
    Chili with Chick-Peas, 72
    Lean Beef Super Supper Sandwiches, 45
    Mini Meat Loaves, 68
    New York Pepper Steak, 74
    Oriental Hot Pot, 118
    Sirloin Steak with Wine and Shallot Sauce, 70
    Stir-Fried Beef with Broccoli, 71
    Warm Calves' Liver Salad, 67
    Warm Steak Salad, 66
Beets, Orange-Glazed, 149
Bisque, Spicy Clamato, 55
Black Butter Sauce, 113
Blue Cheese
    Burgers, 73
    Curly Endive with Walnuts and, 59
    Dip, Creamy, 37
    Topping, 73
Brandied Cranberry Sauce, 159
Bratwurst Skillet Supper, 86
Bread, Pizza, 42
Brie, Sautéed Pears and, 154
Bouillon
    Court, 28
    Tomato, 13
Broccoli
    and Red Onion Soup, 54
    and Tomatoes, Rice with, 142
    Pasta, 134
    Salad with Sunflower Seeds, 61
    Stir-Fried Beef with, 71
Brulée, Fast Fruit, 155
Bulgur and Mushroom Pilaf, 28
Butter Sauce, Black, 113
Button Mushroom Stir-Fry, Asparagus and, 149
Buttermilk Pancakes, Banana, 37

C

Cabbage Skillet Dinner, Beef, 72
Caesar Dressing, Romaine Salad with, 64
California Stuffed Zucchini, 148
Calves' Liver Salad, Warm, 67
Cake
  Dessert French Toast, 152
  Frosted Angel, 156
  Orange-Drizzled Slices, 155
Caramelized Oranges, 155
Caraway Vegetable Platter, 88
Carrots
  Carrot, Celery and Pecan Salad, 59
  Cream of Carrot Soup, 53
  Julienne of Carrots in Honey Glaze, 151
Casseroles
  Beef Noodle Stove-Top, 74
  Jiffy Bean, 146
  Speedy Lentil and Bean, 140
Cauliflower and Tofu Soup, Curried, 52
Celery
  and Pecan Salad, Carrot, 59
  Sauté, Green Bean and, 144
Cheddar Dip, Warm, 37
Cheddar-Soufflé Omelette, 129
Cheese
  Bacon and Swiss Cheese Frittata, 122
  Blue Cheese Topping, 73
  Cheddar-Soufflé Omelette, 129
  Cheese Omelette, 19
  Cheese-Topped Pork Chops, 77
  Creamy Blue Cheese Dip, 37
  Curly Endive with Walnuts and Blue
    Cheese, 59
  Fondue with Italian Flavors, 16
  Gnocchi with Four Cheeses, 135
  Individual Three-Cheese Soufflés, 126
  Mock Cheese Soufflé, 128
  Mozzarella Toasts, 35
  Parmesan Toasts, 9
  Quick Macaroni and Cheese, 139
  Real Welsh Rarebit, 129
  Scrambled Eggs with Cheese, Mushroom
    and Pepper, 124
  Spanish Tortilla, 125
  Three-Pepper Three-Cheese Pizza, 32
  Warm Cheddar Dip, 37
  Warm Nacho Cheese Dip, 37
  Watercress Frittata, 120
Cherry Sauce, Hot, 159
Cherry Tomatoes
  Sautéed Snow Peas and, 149
  with Fresh Basil, Sautéed, 149

Chicken
  and Apple Sauté, 99
  and Red Pepper Stir-Fry, 94
  and Snow Peas in Packets, 31
  Breasts Piccata, 105
  Breasts with Chèvre and Julienne
    Peppers, 107
  Hash, 97
  Normande Sauté, 98
  Sauté with Mushrooms, 98
  Warm Breast of Chicken Salad, 67
Chick-Peas
  Chili with, 72
  Pasta with, 142
  Ratatouille and, 147
Chili
  Beef Burgers, 72
  Chowder, Vegetable, 48
  with Chick-Peas, 72
Chilled Cucumber Soup, 55
Chocolate
  Fondue, 159
  Sauce, Fast, 31
Chowder
  Clam and Corn, 52
  Delicate Salmon with Pasta Shells, 57
  Salmon and Corn, 52
  Tomato-Bean, 50
  Vegetable Chili, 48
Chutney Sauce, Ginger, 119
Cinnamon Orange Compote, 155
Citrus Salmon Salad, 62
Citrus Sections, Warm, 155
Clam
  and Corn Chowder, 52
  Sauce, Fettuccine with Mushroom and,
    139
Clamato Bisque, Spicy, 55
Coleslaw, with Variations, 64
Compote
  Baked Winter, 24
  Cinnamon Orange, 155
Consommé, Mushroom, 52
Coriander-Crumbed Wings and Potato
  Wedges, 102
Country Garden Poached Eggs, 127
Court Bouillon, 28
Couscous, 143
Crab
  and Avocado Salad, Hot, 60
  Salad Croissants with Peaches and
    Pecans, 38
  Vichyssoise, Hearty, 57
Cranberry Sauce, Brandied, 159
Cream of Carrot Soup, 53
Cream of Vegetable Soup, 53
Creamy Blue Cheese Dip, 37
Creole Ham and Rice, 80
Croissants, Crab Salad with Peaches and
  Pecans, 38

Croque-Madame, 45
Croque-Monsieur, 45
Crostini, Garlic Tomato, 34
Croutons, 117
Cucumber
  and Tomato Salsa, Tacos with, 40
  Salad, Hearts of Romaine and, 59
  Salad with Yogurt and Dill, 60
  Soup, Chilled, 55
Curly Endive with Walnuts and Blue
  Cheese, 59
Curried Cauliflower and Tofu Soup, 52
Curried Lamb Chops, 87
Curried Squash Soup, 54
Curry, Hurry, 80

D

Delicate Salmon Chowder with Pasta
  Shells, 57
Dessert French Toast, 152
Desserts
  Applesauce Angel Pudding, 152
  Baked Winter Compote, 24
  Barbecued Banana Boats, 155
  Caramelized Oranges, 155
  Chocolate Fondue, 159
  Cinnamon Orange Compote, 155
  Dessert French Toast, 152
  Fast and Easy Fruit Desserts, 155
  Fast Fruit Brulée, 155
  Fast Fruit Desserts
    Apple, 155
    Cantaloupe, 155
    Fig, 155
    Honeydew Melon, 155
    Mango, 155
    Orange, 155
    Peach Halves, 155
    Peach Slices and Blueberries, 155
    Peach Slices topped with Sweetened
      Yogurt, 155
    Pear, 155
    Pineapple, 155
    Strawberries, 155
  Fast Sauces for Ice Cream
    Brandied Cranberry Sauce, 159
    Fast Chocolate Sauce, 31
    Hot Cherry Sauce, 159
    Mincemeat Sauce, 159
  Fresh Fruit in Yogurt, 158
  Frosted Angel Cake, 156

  Frozen Fruit Yogurt, 158
  Fruit Kabobs, 156
  Grilled Pineapple Kabobs, 155
  Ice Cream Dress-Ups, 156
  Orange-Drizzled Cake Slices, 155
  Peach and Ricotta Parfait, 157
  Sautéed Apple Slices, 155
  Sautéed Pears and Brie, 154
  Souffléed Dessert Omelette, 158
  Speedy Mousse, 15
  Stove-Top Rice Pudding, 156
  Strawberries and Sicilian Cream, 159
  Strawberries Romanoff, 155
  Warm Citrus Sections, 155
  Yogurt Sundae, 155
Dipping Sauces, 77
Dips
  Creamy Blue Cheese Dip, 37
  Hummus, 34
  Peppery Tomato Dip, 102
  Sour Cream Fruit Dip, 155
  Spinach Dip in a Rye Shell, 36
  Warm Cheddar Dip, 37
  Warm Nacho Cheese Dip, 37
Double-Olive Tuna Spread, 39

E

Eggs
  Bacon and Swiss Cheese Frittata, 122
  Basic French Omelette, 19
  Cheddar-Soufflé Omelette, 129
  Cheese Omelette, 19
  Country Garden Poached Eggs, 127
  Frittata in a Skillet, 122
  Herbed Omelette, 19
  Individual Three-Cheese Soufflés, 126
  Light Eggs Benedict with Prosciutto, 123
  Mock Cheese Soufflé, 128
  Poached Eggs, 126
  Roesti Potatoes with Poached Eggs, 126
  Scrambled Eggs with Cheese, Mushroom
    and Pepper, 124
  Scrambled Eggs with Green Onions, 124
  Scrambled Eggs with Tomato, Basil and
    Bacon, 124
  Smoked Fish and Sour Cream Omelette,
    19
  Spanish Tortilla, 125
  Warm Bacon and Egg Salad, 65
  Watercress Frittata, 120
  Zucchini, Potato and Egg Skillet Supper,
    25
Eight Treasure Soup, 55
Endive, Curly, with Walnuts and Blue
  Cheese, 59

F

Fast and Easy Fruit Desserts, 155
Fast Chocolate Sauce, 31
Fast Fruit Brulée, 155
Fast Sauces for Ice Cream, 159
Fettuccine with Mushroom and Clam
    Sauce, 139
Fettuccine and Linguine with Spring Leeks
    and Zucchini, 138
Fillet of Sole with Green Grapes, 113
Fish
    Almond-Breaded Fillets, 112
    Baked Haddock Fillets with Cheese, 113
    Baked Salmon Salad, 117
    Baked Whitefish with Mustard-Dill
        Sauce, 114
    Double-Olive Tuna Spread, 39
    Fillet of Sole with Green Grapes, 113
    Fish Fillets in Packets, 110
    Fish Fillets with Lime-Ginger Sauce, 114
    Linguine with Smoked Salmon, 133
    Oriental Fish Fillets, 108
    Oven-Poached Salmon in Dill Sauce, 111
    Parmesan Fish Fingers with Lemon, 13
    Rotini with Salmon and Chives, 133
    Salmon Pat-a-Cakes with Quick Tartar
        Sauce, 110
    Smoked Fish and Sour Cream Omelette,
        19
    Sole with Black Butter, 113
    Steamed Salmon Fillets, 28
    Tomato Linguine with Salmon, 132
Fondue
    Chocolate, 159
    with Italian Flavors, 16
French Omelette, Basic, 19
French Toast
    Dessert, 152
    with Pesto, 38
Fresh Fruit in Yogurt, 158
Fresh Minted Salsa, 90
Fried Tomatoes, 151
Frittata
    Bacon and Swiss Cheese, 122
    in a Skillet, 122
    Watercress, 120
Frosted Angel Cake, 156
Frozen Fruit Yogurt, 158
Fruit
    Brulée, Fast, 155
    Desserts, Fast and Easy, 155
    Dip, Sour Cream, 155
    in Yogurt, Fresh, 158
    Yogurt, Frozen, 158
Fusilli with Tomato-Vegetable Primavera,
    137

G

Garlic Croutons, 117
Garlic Tomato Crostini, 34
Ginger Chutney Sauce, 119
Gnocchi with Four Cheeses, 135
Grains, etc.
    Bulgur and Mushroom Pilaf, 28
    Couscous, 143
    Orange Rice and Red Lentil Pilaf, 143
    Parsley-Lemon Rice, 140
    Rice Pilaf, 143
    Rice with Broccoli and Tomatoes, 142
    Speedy Lentil and Bean Casserole, 140
Grapes
    Fillet of Sole with Green Grapes, 113
    Frosted, 148
Green Beans
    Green Bean and Celery Sauté, 144
    in Mustard Vinaigrette, Jarlsberg and,
        151
    with Garlic and Sesame Seeds, 146
Green Peppercorn Chicken Sauté, 98
Grilled Lamb Chops with Herb Butter, 90
Grilled Pineapple Kabobs, 155

H

Haddock Fillets, Baked with Cheese, 113
Ham
    and Rice, Creole, 80
    and Vegetable Bean Soup, Hearty, 51
Hamburgers
    Blue Cheese, 73
    Chili Beef, 72
    Open-Faced, 47
    with Sour Cream Sauce, 72
Hash, Chicken, 97
Hearts of Romaine and Cucumber Salad,
    59
Hearty Crab Vichyssoise, 57
Hearty Ham and Vegetable Bean Soup, 51
Herb Butter, 90
Herbed Croutons, 117
Herbed Omelette, 19
Herb-Grilled Turkey Scallopini, 23
Hollandaise Sauce, Light, 123
Honey-Soy Glaze, Lamb Chops with, 88
Horseradish Dressing, 67
Hot Cherry Sauce, 159
Hot Crab and Avocado Salad, 60
Hummus, 34
Hurry Curry, 80

I

Ice Cream
  Dress-Ups, 156
  Fast Sauces for, 159
Individual Three-Cheese Soufflés, 126
Italian-Style Chicken, 101

J

Jarlsberg and Green Beans in Mustard
    Vinaigrette, 151
Jiffy Bean Casserole, 146
Julienne of Carrots in Honey Glaze, 151

K

Kabobs
  Fruit, 156
  Grilled Pineapple, 155
  Pork and Red Pepper Shish Kabobs, 83
Kiwi, Pork Cutlets with, 83

L

Lamb
  Curried Lamb Chops, 87
  Grilled Lamb Chops with Herb Butter, 90
  Lamb Chops Creole, 88
  Lamb Chops with Honey-Soy Glaze, 88
  Lamb Hot Pot, 91
  Lamb Patties in Pita Rounds, 90
  Medallions of Lamb in Red Wine Sauce,
    27
  Schnitzelled Chops or Chicken, 92
Lean Beef Super Supper Sandwiches, 45
Leeks
  and Lemon Marmalade, Veal Chops with,
    114
  and Zucchini, Linguine and Fettuccine
    with, 138
  Leek and Cream Filling for Omelette, 19
Lemon
  Chicken, 98
  Cream Sauce, Poached Turkey Breast
    with, 106
  Lemon-Basil Chicken Strips, 20
  Shrimp with Fresh Vegetables, 116

Lentils
  Orange Rice and Red Lentil Pilaf, 143
  Speedy Lentil and Bean Casserole, 140
Light Eggs Benedict with Prosciutto, 123
Light Hollandaise Sauce, 123
Linguine
  and Fettuccine with Spring Leeks and
    Zucchini, 138
  with Fresh Tomatoes and Seafood, 8
  with Salmon, Tomato, 132
  with Smoked Salmon, 133
Liver
  Salad, Warm Calves', 67
  with Yogurt-Mustard Sauce, Baby Beef,
    75

M

Macaroni and Cheese, Quick, 139
Marsala Chicken Sauté, 98
Meat Loaves, Mini, 68
Medallions of Lamb in Red Wine Sauce, 27
Mediterranean Salad, 67
Mincemeat Sauce, 159
Mini Meat Loaves, 68
Minted Salsa, Fresh, 90
Mock Cheese Soufflé, 128
Monte Cristo, 45
Mousse, Speedy, 15
Mozzarella Toasts, 35
Muffulettas, 43
Mussels with Garlic and Tomatoes, 119
Mustard
  Chicken Sauté, 98
  Cream, 87
  Mustard-Dill Sauce, Baked Whitefish
    with, 114
Mushrooms
  and Clam Sauce, Fettuccine with, 139
  and Mozzarella Pizza, 42
  Asparagus and Button Mushroom Stir-Fry,
    149
  Chicken Sauté with, 98
  Consommé, 52
  Pilaf, Bulgur and, 28
  Tomato Mushroom Soup with Rye
    Croutons, 56
  Veal Scallopini in Mushroom Madeira
    Sauce, 92

N

Nacho Cheese Dip, Warm, 37
New York Pepper Steak, 74

O

Olive
  and Onion Salad, Orange, 64
  Double-Olive Tuna Spread, 39
  Salad, 43
Omelette
  Basic French, 19
  Cheddar-Soufflé, 129
  Cheese, 19
  Herbed, 19
  Leek and Cream Filling for, 19
  Provençale Filling for, 19
  Smoked Fish and Sour Cream, 19
  Souffléed Dessert, 158
One Potato—Two Potato and Chops, 78
Onions
  and Apples, Bangers with, 85
  Broccoli and Red Onion Soup, 54
  Orange, Olive and Onion Salad, 64
  Romaine and Red Onion Salad, 26
  Saucy Chicken with Green Onions, 96
  Scrambled Eggs with Green Onions, 124
Open-Faced Hamburgers, 47
Open-Faced Steak Sandwich with
  Mushroom Sauce, 47
Oranges
  Caramelized, 155
  Cinnamon Orange Compote, 155
  Orange-Drizzled Cake Slices, 155
  Orange-Glazed Beets, 149
  Orange, Olive and Onion Salad, 64
  Orange Rice and Red Lentil Pilaf, 143
Oriental Fish Fillets, 108
Oriental Hot Pot, 118
Orzo, Parsley-Lemon, 140
Oven-Poached Salmon in Dill Sauce, 111

P

Pancakes
  Banana Buttermilk, 37
  Potato-Zucchini, 150
Parfait, Peach and Ricotta, 157
Parmesan
  Chicken Fingers with Lemon, 13
  Fish Fingers with Lemon, 13
  Rotini, 20
  Toasts, 9
Parsley-Lemon Orzo, 140
Parsley-Lemon Rice, 140

Pasta
  Broccoli Pasta, 134
  Fusilli with Tomato-Vegetable Primavera,
    137
  Gnocchi with Four Cheeses, 135
  Linguine and Fettuccine with Spring Leeks
    and Zucchini, 138
  Linguine with Fresh Tomatoes and
    Seafood, 8
  Linguine with Smoked Salmon, 133
  Parmesan Rotini, 20
  Parsley-Lemon Orzo, 140
  Pasta Shells with Red Pepper and Parsley
    Sauce, 130
  Pasta with Artichokes and Pine Nuts, 141
  Pasta with Chick-Peas, 142
  Penne with Sweet Peppers and Two
    Cheeses, 136
  Quick Macaroni and Cheese, 139
  Rotini with Salmon and Chives, 133
  Spaghetti Carbonara, 135
  Spaghetti with Sausage and Tomato
    Sauce, 133
  Tomato Linguine with Salmon, 132
  Tortellini in Cream Sauce, 139
  Two-Pepper Pasta with Prosciutto, 136
  Warm Pasta Seafood Salad, 61
Peaches
  Peach and Ricotta Parfait, 157
  Peaches and Pecans, Crab Salad
    Croissants with, 38
Pears
  and Brie, Sautéed, 154
  in Wine, 82
  Pink, Pork Chops with, 83
Penne with Sweet Peppers and Two
  Cheeses, 136
Peppers
  Beef Paillards with Double Pepper Sauce,
    71
  Chicken and Red Pepper Stir-Fry, 94
  Chicken Breasts with Chèvre and Julienne
    Peppers, 107
  Pasta Shells with Red Pepper and Parsley
    Sauce, 130
  Penne with Sweet Peppers and Two
    Cheeses, 136
  Pork and Red Pepper Shish Kabobs, 83
  Three-Pepper Three-Cheese Pizza, 32
  Two-Pepper Pasta with Prosciutto, 136
Peppery Tomato Dip, 102
Pesto, French Toast with, 38
Pilaf
  Bulgur and Mushroom, 28
  Orange Rice and Red Lentil, 143
  Rice, 143
Pineapple Kabobs, Grilled, 155
Pizza
  Bread, 42
  Mushroom and Mozzarella, 42
  Three-Pepper Three-Cheese, 32

Poached Eggs, 126
Poached Eggs, Country Garden, 127
Poached Eggs, Roesti Potatoes with, 126
Poached Turkey Breast with Lemon Cream
    Sauce, 106
Pork
    Bangers with Onions and Apples, 85
    Bratwurst Skillet Supper, 86
    Cheese-Topped Pork Chops, 77
    Creole Ham and Rice, 80
    Hurry Curry, 80
    One Potato—Two Potato and Chops, 78
    Oriental Hot Pot, 118
    Pork and Red Pepper Shish Kabobs, 83
    Pork Chops in Beer with Sauerkraut, 78
    Pork Chops with Pink Pears, 82
    Pork Cutlets with Kiwi, 83
    Pork Medallions with Cranberry-Port
        Sauce, 84
    Pork Tenderloin with Mustard and Herbs,
        85
    Pork Tenderloin with Mustard-Peppercorn
        Crust, 81
    Sausage Patties with Mustard Cream, 87
    Schnitzelled Chops or Chicken, 92
    Spanish Tortilla, 125
Potato-Zucchini Pancakes, 150
Potatoes
    Coriander-Crumbed Wings and Potato
        Wedges, 102
    One Potato—Two Potato and Chops, 78
    Potato-Zucchini Pancakes, 150
    Roesti Potatoes with Poached Eggs, 126
    Zucchini, Potato and Egg Skillet Supper,
        25
Poultry
    Chicken and Apple Sauté, 99
    Chicken and Red Pepper Stir-Fry, 94
    Chicken and Snow Peas in Packets, 31
    Chicken Breasts Piccata, 105
    Chicken Breasts with Chèvre and Julienne
        Peppers, 107
    Chicken Hash, 97
    Chicken Normande Sauté, 98
    Chicken Sauté with Mushrooms, 98
    Coriander-Crumbed Wings and Potato
        Wedges, 102
    Green Peppercorn Chicken Sauté, 98
    Herb-Grilled Turkey Scallopini, 23
    Italian-Style Chicken, 101
    Lemon-Basil Chicken Strips, 20
    Lemon Chicken, 98
    Marsala Chicken Sauté, 98
    Mustard Chicken Sauté, 98
    Oriental Hot Pot, 118
    Parmesan Chicken Fingers with Lemon, 13
    Poached Turkey Breast with Lemon Cream
        Sauce, 106
    Raspberry Chicken, 102
    Raspberry Vinegar Chicken Sauté, 98

    Rosemary and Mustard Glazed Chicken,
        11
    Saucy Chicken with Green Onions, 96
    Schnitzelled Chops or Chicken, 92
    Stir-Fried Chicken and Snow Peas, 96
    Succotash Stew, 105
    Sunny Citrus Chicken, 100
    Tropical Chicken, 101
    Turkey Cutlets with Lemon and Rosemary,
        107
    Warm Breast of Chicken Salad, 67
Prosciutto
    Light Eggs Benedict with, 123
    Two-Pepper Pasta with, 136
Pudding
    Applesauce Angel, 152
    Stove-Top Rice, 156

Q

Quick Macaroni and Cheese, 139
Quick Tartar Sauce, 110

R

Rarebit, Real Welsh, 129
Raspberry Chicken, 102
Raspberry Vinegar Chicken Sauté, 98
Ratatouille and Chick-Peas, 147
Real Welsh Rarebit, 129
Red Onion Soup, Broccoli and, 54
Rice
    Orange Rice and Red Lentil Pilaf, 143
    Parsley-Lemon Rice, 140
    Rice Pilaf, 143
    Rice with Broccoli and Tomatoes, 142
    Stove-Top Rice Pudding, 156
Ricotta Parfait, Peach and, 157
Roesti Potatoes with Poached Eggs, 126
Romaine
    and Cucumber Salad, Hearts of, 59
    and Red Onion Salad, 26
    Salad with Caesar Dressing, 64
    Salad with Horseradish Dressing, Spinach
        and, 67
Rosemary and Mustard Glazed Chicken,
    11
Rotini
    Parmesan, 20
    with Salmon and Chives, 133
Rum and Sour Cream Sauce, 154

S

Salad Dressings
  Caesar Dressing, 64
  Classic Vinaigrette, 22
  Creamy Vinaigrette, 22
  Dressing for Warm Pasta Seafood Salad,
    61
  Horseradish Dressing, 67
  Italian-Flavored Vinaigrette, 22
  Mustard Vinaigrette, 151
  Tomato Vinaigrette, 22
  Yogurt-Garlic Dressing, 59
Salads
  Artichoke Salad in Romaine Boats, 58
  Avocado and Walnut Salad, 67
  Baked Salmon Salad, 117
  Broccoli Salad with Sunflower Seeds, 61
  Carrot, Celery and Pecan Salad, 59
  Citrus Salmon Salad, 62
  Coleslaw, with Variations, 64
  Crab Salad Croissants with Peaches and
    Pecans, 38
  Cucumber Salad with Yogurt and Dill, 60
  Curly Endive with Walnuts and Blue
    Cheese, 59
  Hearts of Romaine and Cucumber Salad,
    59
  Hot Crab and Avocado Salad, 60
  Mediterranean Salad, 67
  Olive Salad, 43
  Orange, Olive and Onion Salad, 64
  Romaine and Red Onion Salad, 26
  Romaine Salad with Caesar Dressing, 64
  Skillet Chicken Salad, 62
  Spinach and Romaine Salad with
    Horseradish Dressing, 67
  Tomato Salad, 38
  Warm Bacon and Egg Salad, 65
  Warm Breast of Chicken Salad, 67
  Warm Calves' Liver Salad, 67
  Warm Mexican Salad, 63
  Warm Pasta Seafood Salad, 61
  Warm Scallop Salad, 67
  Warm Steak Salad, 66
Salmon
  and Chives, Rotini with, 133
  and Corn Chowder, 52
  Chowder with Pasta Shells, Delicate, 57
  Fillets, Steamed, 28
  Oven-Poached in Dill Sauce, 111
  Pat-a-Cakes with Quick Tartar Sauce,
    110
  Salad, Baked, 117
  Salad, Citrus, 62
  Smoked, Linguine with, 133
  Tomato Linguine with, 132
Salsa
  Fresh Minted, 90
  Tomato and Cucumber, Tacos with, 40

Sandwiches
  Avocado Melts, 46
  Crab Salad Croissants with Peaches and
    Pecans, 38
  Croque-Madame, 45
  Croque-Monsieur, 45
  French Toast with Pesto, 38
  Lean Beef Super Supper Sandwiches, 45
  Monte Cristo, 45
  Muffulettas, 43
  Open-Faced Hamburgers, 47
  Open-Faced Steak Sandwich with
    Mushroom Sauce, 47
  Pizza Bread, 42
  Tacos with Tomato and Cucumber Salsa,
    40
  Tongue Croque-Monsieur, 45
Sauces, Dessert
  Brandied Cranberry Sauce, 159
  Fast Chocolate Sauce, 31
  Hot Cherry Sauce, 159
  Mincemeat Sauce, 159
  Rum and Sour Cream Sauce, 154
  Sicilian Cream, 159
Sauces, Savory
  Barbecue Sauce, 68
  Black Butter Sauce, 113
  Cranberry-Port Sauce, 84
  Dipping Sauces, 77
  Double Pepper Sauce, 71
  Fresh Minted Salsa, 90
  Ginger Chutney Sauce, 119
  Light Hollandaise Sauce, 123
  Lime-Ginger Sauce, 114
  Mustard-Dill Sauce, 114
  Pesto, 38
  Quick Tartar Sauce, 110
  Sour Cream Sauce, 72
  Tomato and Cucumber Salsa, 40
Saucy Chicken with Green Onions, 96
Sauerkraut, Pork Chops in Beer with, 78
Sausage and Tomato Sauce, Spaghetti
  with, 133
Sausage Patties with Mustard Cream, 87
Sautéed Apple Slices, 155
Sautéed Cherry Tomatoes with Fresh Basil,
  149
Sautéed Pears and Brie, 154
Sautéed Snow Peas and Cherry Tomatoes,
  149
Savory Vegetable Ring, 144
Scallopini
  Herb-Grilled Turkey, 23
  Veal, in Mushroom and Madeira Sauce,
    92
Scallops
  and Broccoli with Almonds, 117
  Provençale, 119
  Warm Scallop Salad, 67

Schnitzelled Chops or Chicken, 92
Scrambled Eggs with Green Onions, 124
Seafood
    Lemon Shrimp with Fresh Vegetables, 116
    Linguine with Fresh Tomatoes and
      Seafood, 8
    Mussels with Garlic and Tomatoes, 119
    Oriental Hot Pot, 118
    Scallops and Broccoli with Almonds, 117
    Scallops Provençale, 119
    Warm Pasta Seafood Salad, 61
    Warm Scallop Salad, 67
Shrimp, Lemon with Fresh Vegetables, 116
Sicilian Cream, Strawberries and, 159
Sirloin Steak with Wine and Shallot Sauce,
    70
Smoked Fish and Sour Cream Omelette, 19
Snow Peas
    and Cherry Tomatoes, Sautéed, 149
    in Packets, Chicken and, 31
    Stir-Fried Chicken and, 96
Sole with Black Butter, 113
Souffléed Dessert Omelette, 158
Soufflés
    Individual Three-Cheese, 126
    Mock Cheese, 128
    Omelette, Cheddar, 129
Soups
    Bean and Bacon Soup, 50
    Broccoli and Red Onion Soup, 54
    Chilled Cucumber Soup, 55
    Clam and Corn Chowder, 52
    Cream of Carrot Soup, 53
    Cream of Vegetable Soup, 53
    Curried Cauliflower and Tofu Soup, 52
    Curried Squash Soup, 54
    Delicate Salmon Chowder with Pasta
      Shells, 57
    Eight Treasure Soup, 55
    Hearty Crab Vichyssoise, 57
    Hearty Ham and Vegetable Bean Soup,
      51
    Mushroom Consommé, 52
    Salmon and Corn Chowder, 52
    Spa Vegetable Soup, 56
    Spicy Clamato Bisque, 55
    Tomato-Bean Chowder, 50
    Tomato Bouillon, 13
    Tomato Mushroom Soup with Rye
      Croutons, 56
    Vegetable Chili Chowder, 48
Sour Cream
    Fruit Dip, 155
    Sauce, Burgers with, 72
    Sauce, Rum and, 154
Spa Vegetable Soup, 56
Spaghetti Carbonara, 135
Spaghetti with Sausage and Tomato Sauce,
    133
Spanish Tortilla, 125
Speedy Lentil and Bean Casserole, 140

Speedy Mousse, 15
Spicy Clamato Bisque, 55
Spinach and Romaine Salad with
    Horseradish Dressing, 67
Spinach Dip in a Rye Shell, 36
Squash Soup, Curried, 54
Steak
    New York Pepper, 74
    Open-Faced Steak Sandwich with
      Mushroom Sauce, 47
    Salad, Warm, 66
    Sirloin, with Wine and Shallot Sauce, 70
Steamed Salmon Fillets, 28
Stew, Succotash, 105
Stir-Fried Beef with Broccoli, 71
Stir-Fried Chicken and Snow Peas, 96
Stove-Top Rice Pudding, 156
Strawberries and Sicilian Cream, 159
Strawberries Romanoff, 155
Succotash Stew, 105
Sunny Citrus Salad, 100

T

Tacos with Tomato and Cucumber Salsa, 40
Tartar Sauce, Quick, 110
Three-Pepper Three-Cheese Pizza, 32
Toasts
    Mozzarella, 35
    Parmesan, 9
Tofu Soup, Curried Cauliflower and, 52
Tomatoes
    Fried, 151
    Fusilli with Tomato-Vegetable Primavera,
      137
    Garlic Tomato Crostini, 34
    Linguine with Fresh Tomatoes and
      Seafood, 8
    Mussels with Garlic and, 119
    Peppery Tomato Dip, 102
    Rice with Broccoli and, 142
    Sautéed Cherry Tomatoes with Fresh
      Basil, 149
    Sautéed Snow Peas and Cherry
      Tomatoes, 149
    Scrambled Eggs with Tomato, Basil and
      Bacon, 124
    Tomato and Cucumber Salsa, 40
    Tomato-Bean Chowder, 50
    Tomato Bouillon, 13
    Tomato Linguine with Salmon, 132
    Tomato Mushroom Soup with Rye
      Croutons, 56
    Tomato Salad, 38

Tongue Croque-Monsieur, 45
Tortellini in Cream Sauce, 139
Tropical Chicken, 101
Tuna Spread, Double-Olive, 39
Turkey
   Breast, Poached, with Lemon Cream
      Sauce, 106
   Cutlets with Lemon and Rosemary, 107
   Scallopini, Herb-Grilled, 23
Two-Pepper Pasta with Prosciutto, 136

V

Veal
   Schnitzelled Chops or Chicken, 92
   Veal Chops with Green Peppercorns, 93
   Veal Scallopini in Mushroom Madeira
      Sauce, 92
   Veal Scallops with Leeks and Lemon
      Marmalade, 14
Vegetable Bean Soup, Hearty Ham and, 51
Vegetable Chili Chowder, 48
Vegetable Sauté, 146
Vegetable Soup, Cream of, 53
Vegetable Soup, Spa, 56
Vegetables
   Asparagus and Button Mushroom Stir-Fry,
      149
   Broccoli Pasta, 134
   California Stuffed Zucchini, 148
   Caraway Vegetable Platter, 88
   Country Garden Poached Eggs, 127
   Fried Tomatoes, 151
   Fusilli with Tomato-Vegetable Primavera,
      137
   Green Bean and Celery Sauté, 144
   Green Beans with Garlic and Sesame
      Seeds, 146
   Jarlsberg and Green Beans in Mustard
      Vinaigrette, 151
   Jiffy Bean Casserole, 146
   Julienne of Carrots in Honey Glaze, 151
   Linguine and Fettuccine with Spring Leeks
      and Zucchini, 138
   One Potato—Two Potato and Chops, 78
   Orange-Glazed Carrots, 149
   Potato-Zucchini Pancakes, 150
   Ratatouille and Chick-Peas, 147
   Roesti Potatoes with Poached Eggs, 126
   Sautéed Cherry Tomatoes with Fresh
      Basil, 149
   Sautéed Snow Peas and Cherry
      Tomatoes, 149

Savory Vegetable Ring, 144
Speedy Lentil and Bean Casserole, 140
Vegetable Sauté, 146
Zucchini, Potato and Egg Skillet Supper,
   25
Vichyssoise, Hearty Crab, 57
Vinaigrette for Greens, 22

W

Walnuts
   and Blue Cheese, Curly Endive with, 59
   Avocado and Walnut Salad, 67
Warm Bacon and Egg Salad, 65
Warm Breast of Chicken Salad, 67
Warm Calves' Liver Salad, 67
Warm Cheddar Dip, 37
Warm Citrus Sections, 155
Warm Mexican Salad, 63
Warm Nacho Cheese Dip, 37
Warm Pasta Seafood Salad, 61
Warm Scallop Salad, 67
Warm Steak Salad, 66
Watercress Frittata, 120
Welsh Rarebit, Real, 129
Whitefish, Baked, with Mustard-Dill Sauce,
   114

Y

Yogurt
   and Dill, Cucumber Salad with, 60
   Fresh Fruit in, 158
   Frozen Fruit, 158
   Sundae, 155
   Yogurt-Garlic Dressing, 59
   Yogurt-Mustard Sauce, Baby Beef Liver
      with, 75

Z

Zucchini
   California Stuffed, 148
   Linguine and Fettuccine with Spring Leeks
      and, 138
   Potato-Zucchini Pancakes, 150
   Zucchini, Potato and Egg Skillet Supper,
      25

The Canadian Living Cookbook

by Carol Ferguson and the food writers of Canadian Living *Magazine*

A bestselling full-color cookbook featuring more than 525 delicious, carefully tested recipes for all occasions. Enticing theme menus highlight the regional foods of Canada and over 200 sumptuous photographs and dozens of helpful hints, charts and step-by-step features make this a book that no Canadian cook should be without.

$34.95 (hardcover)

The Canadian Living Microwave Cookbook

by Margaret Fraser and the food writers of Canadian Living *Magazine*

At last, a book that shows you how to make the most of your marvelous microwave! Here's a complete one-volume microwave guide with more than 175 easy-to-prepare recipes, ten timesaving theme menus, over 80 full-color photographs and dozens of hints and ideas.

$24.95 (hardcover)

Canadian Living Glorious Christmas Crafts

by Anna Hobbs and the craft editors of Canadian Living *Magazine*

From the pages of *Canadian Living* comes this treasury of over 135 favorite crafts for the holiday season. Here are imaginative projects for those who like to stitch, quilt, embroider, knit, cut and paste, or work with wood and paint. Dozens of full-color photographs and easy-to-follow diagrams and instructions guarantee success for everyone from beginner to expert.

$24.95 (hardcover)

The Canadian Living Barbecue and Summer Foods Cookbook

by Margaret Fraser and the food writers of Canadian Living *Magazine*

Featuring over 175 recipes and ten menus illustrated by more than 80 mouth-watering photographs, this cookbook shows you how to make the most of the summer season. Up-to-date information on equipment and barbecuing techniques makes this the most complete cookbook for the outdoor cook.

$19.95 (softcover)

A Year of Canadian Living Diary

From the editors of *Canadian Living* comes this beautiful desk diary celebrating the Canadian year. For every season, there are wonderful ideas for food and crafts, family activities, decorating and entertaining illustrated by over 100 colorful and evocative photographs.

$15.95 (hardcover in slipcase)

Design and Art Direction: Gordon Sibley Design Inc.

Editorial: Hugh Brewster
Catherine Fraccaro

Editorial Assistance: Beverley Renahan
Deborah Viets

Production: Susan Barrable

Production Assistance: Catherine A. Clark

Typography: Attic Typesetting Inc.

Color Separation: La Cromolito

Printing and Binding: New Interlitho S.p.A.

Canadian Living
Advisory Board: Robert A. Murray
Carol Ferguson
Margaret Fraser

THE CANADIAN LIVING RUSH-HOUR COOKBOOK
was produced by Madison Press Books
under the direction of Albert E. Cummings.